LETTERS FROM KIEV

LETTERS FROM KIEV

Solomea Pavlychko
Translated by Myrna Kostash

with a preface and annotations by
Bohdan Krawchenko

St. Martin's Press
New York

in association with the Canadian Institute
of Ukrainian Studies Press, University of Alberta

Scholarly and Reference Division,
St. Martin's Press, Inc., 175 Fifth Avenue,
New York, NY 10010

First published in the United States of America 1992

Printed in the United States of America

ISBN 0-312-07588-X

Library of Congress Cataloguing-in-Publication Data

Pavlychko, S. D. (Solomiia Dmitrievna)

Letters from Kiev / Solomea Pavlychko : translated by
Myrna Kostash ; with a preface and annotations by
Bohdan Krawchenko.

p.   cm.

ISBN 0-312-07588-X

1. Ukraine—Politics and government—1945–1991. 2. Ukraine—Politics
and government—1991– 3. Pavlycho, S. D. (Solomiia Dmitrievna)
—Correspondence. I. Title.
DK508.848.P38   1992
947'.71084—dc20   92-24086
                                                  CIP

Contents

List of Illustrations

10. *The Kiev Institute of the National Economy contingent at the student hunger strike camp on October Revolution Square (now Independence Square), October 1990.* (Serhii Supinsky)

11. *Meeting on October Revolution Square (now Independence Square), October 1990.* (Serhii Supinsky)

12. *The student hunger strike ends, October 1990.* (Serhii Supinsky)

13. *Picket near St. Sophia Cathedral blocking the arrival of the Moscow Patriarch, Aleksii, October 29, 1990.* (Pavlo Pashchenko)

14. *Demonstrators protesting the arrival of the Moscow Patriarch, Aleksii, near St. Sophia Cathedral, October 29, 1990.* (Pavlo Pashchenko)

15. *Parliamentary session. Communist deputies stand in protest.* (Slavko Maievsky)

16. *Parliamentary session. Communist deputies* (left) *confront deputies from Lviv* (right). (Slavko Maievsky)

Preface

The idea for *Letters from Kiev* grew out a casual conversation in the final week of Solomea Pavlychko's stay in Edmonton, Canada, where she was visiting professor from January to April 1990. Saying good-bye, I urged her to write me a detailed letter on her return. When the first letter arrived, it was obvious that were she to continue, these letters would offer an important eyewitness account of the immense drama unfolding in Ukraine. Encouraged by many telephone calls (and spurred by the need to master the computer that she brought with her to Kiev), she wrote from May 12, 1990 to March 25, 1991. The letters that make up this volume chronicle the clash of political forces, shifting public moods, and private struggles on the eve of the collapse of the USSR and communist rule. They offer a unique perspective on life in Kiev, Ukraine's capital.

Solomea Pavlychko writes as a political insider. She works at the Institute of Literature of the Ukrainian Academy of Sciences, which was a hotbed of oppositional activity. Her father, Dmytro Pavlychko, was and is one of Ukraine's ablest opposition members of parliament. Her letters thus give a center-stage view of the political crises of that fateful year. When she wrote the letters, she had just discovered feminism, and this informs her view of social relations and the politics of everyday life. Finally, as a thirty-three-year-old, she echoes the voice of a new generation that has traveled an enormous distance in freeing the mind and spirit.

The account in this volume begins at a time when the basic political forces had taken shape. The April 1986 Chernobyl tragedy served as a catalyst to rally public opinion against the latest outrages of the regime. Scores of unofficial groups, which had formed in 1986, had by September 1989 united in Rukh, Ukraine's popular front. In January 1990 Rukh demonstrated its political potential when it organized a human chain involving almost a million people linking arms from Kiev to Western Ukraine. The March 1990 elections saw the opposition gain a voice in parliament and ensured that this new institution would play a decisive role in the year ahead. The miners' strike in the summer of 1990 revealed widespread discontent in Ukraine's industrial heartland.

Yet, when Solomea Pavlychko returned to Kiev, conservative forces in society had not given up hope that they could restore the status quo ante. Indeed, throughout the autumn of 1990, in concert with the major provocations that Moscow unleashed in the Baltics, steps were taken in Ukraine to roll back the challenge to communist authority. This conservative backlash poured cold water on the euphoria over the adoption of Ukraine's declaration of sovereignty in July 1990. Resistance to this strategy came from a totally unexpected quarter—Ukraine's students. The student movement that unfolded in the early days of October 1990 carried out some of the most remarkable mass actions Ukraine had ever seen. The events of autumn 1990, described vividly in the letters, were a sobering experience for Ukraine's political elite and hastened the rise of a more moderate leadership headed by Leonid Kravchuk, Ukraine's future president.

Fortunately, the story has a happy ending. On August 24, 1991, in the wake of the failed putsch, Ukraine proclaimed its independence, and two days later parliament banned the Communist Party of Ukraine. Independence was overwhelmingly confirmed by the December 1, 1991 referendum, and that month, the USSR ceased to exist. Some of the oppositionists mentioned in the letters now occupy important posts and play a direct role in forging a democratic and independent Ukraine. Other *dramatis personae* have faded from the scene, and some of them, such as Yazov, Kriuchkov and Lukianov, are facing trial for their role in the coup.

That Ukraine, a country with a tortuous past, achieved independence and democracy without the loss of a single life borders on the miraculous. Ukraine is a colossus among the former Soviet republics: with 53 million people it accounts for

25 to 30 per cent of the former USSR's gross domestic product. More than 12 million Russians inhabit the republic. If the transition to independence was relatively peaceful, and unaccompanied by inter-ethnic strife, this was due in large part to the maturity of the Ukrainian national movement. The struggle for national revival was successfully merged with the fight for democracy, so that the national and democratic movements coincided, unlike what has happened in some other republics.

Independent Ukraine faces formidable challenges. The economy is in crisis and the damage to the environment will take several generations to repair. But Ukraine's greatest asset is her people. The letters provide insight into what motivated many of them during the recent stormy events. Despite the sense of powerlessness and the ever-present dread that the forces of reaction can still emerge victorious, they stood by their individual commitment not to turn back. One hopes that the new Ukraine will harness the human potential which the communist regime so criminally squandered.

Bohdan Krawchenko
Edmonton, Canada
February 1992

May 12, 1990

Dear Bohdan,

I'm writing to you as promised. You just might be interested in reading something about our situation. But, first of all, thank you for the warm welcome in Edmonton. It's only now that I understand how much I enjoyed being with all of you. On my first day at work, the personnel manager of the Institute of Literature literally bawled me out. How could I have gone off to Canada without receiving permission from the executive board of the Academy of Sciences? I had obtained my passport at the Writers' Union. In retaliation, a clerk at the Academy instructed our directors to cancel my sabbatical salary while I was abroad, and this my friends (institute director) Dzeverin and (his deputy) Zhulynsky meekly carried out. The Academy also sent a protest to the Writers' Union and even drew up a telegram to me in Edmonton demanding that I return immediately and render an explanation. But for some reason they never sent it. So I am reminded that I am not a professor, as I was in Edmonton, but a serf, as in the times of Shevchenko.[1] Similarly, no one is interested in my "notable" achievements in Edmonton. Your advice to me to write everything down was gratuitous. The director doesn't give a damn. His deputy, Zhulynsky, has come back from Italy and, as far as I can see, is angling for a position as a corresponding member of the Academy.

The elections to the Academy—yet another farce—will be held on the 17th. Four names have been put forward for two places in the Language and Literature Division: Oliinyk,[2] Zatonsky, Verves and my father, Dmytro Pavlychko.[3] Five members vote. For the single spot as corresponding member, Zhulynsky, Dziuba,[4] Kononenko and Yatsenko are in the running. My director spent half an hour explaining to me how important it is to be an academician; that it means immortality, which is to say that he, along with his mates Novychenko, Kondufor and others, who obtained their posts because they supported the regime, are among the immortals. How can one speak seriously about such things?

In Kiev rather big changes are making themselves felt. They're selling Ukrainian, Belorussian, and Jewish samizdat[5] under a blue-and-yellow flag[6] hanging from a pole on the main street—Khreshchatyk. There is an anti-Gorbachev tone to the articles. A flag flies atop the Rukh[7] building, and in the museum alley beside it you find information booths, photographs, and the guys from the Union of Ukrainian Youth selling their literature. On April 22, in Kiev, the Union organized something very shocking. They laid a wreath of thorns at the Lenin monument, then burned his books. Apparently there were masses of people there, but different versions are circulating. According to a lot of people, the democrat Pohribny failed in his bid to become mayor of Kiev because of this incident. So now we don't have a mayor. Forces split in half, the "right" pushing for their apparatchik, the "left" for Pohribny. (The latter has recently quit the Communist party.) Now other candidates are being put forward and everything is starting all over again.

Morale is low. Everyone criticizes everything, yet at the same time people are apathetic. A faction of left-wing communists has formed within the party, but few have joined up with them. In our institute, the left-wing communists are the most cynical and lazy, and some have a dubious past. Out of 80 communists, their circle has 20. At the all-Union level, the rector of the Moscow Higher Party School heads up the left-wing communists. A Russian Communist party has also been formed under the leadership of the former editor of the journal *Kommunist*, Richard Kosolapov. Both leaders, as their interviews attest, are worried about the preservation of the "state" (I'm sure you know which one they mean). Some people are going about with their declarations of resignation in their heads, but they say they are waiting for the party congress. Essentially they are afraid—for some it's only a couple of years until their pensions, others are angling for a position, and some hope to go abroad. At the same time there are those, like me, who expect nothing. Briukhovetsky[8] and I and a couple of others will announce our decision at the institute party organization meeting on May 18.

Do you remember how, in Edmonton, we mulled over the resignation of some writers from the party—too soon? timely? too late? In fact, it's difficult to sense the atmosphere from such a distance. It's quite heavy here, as before a storm. Some people are in despair, others are demoralized, still others criticize everything, whispering among themselves. Servility is alive and well.

The most terrifying facts concerning radiation levels in Kiev have come to light. The Geology Institute has drawn up a chart of the "hot spots" around Kiev of cesium alone. There are 145 of them where the dosage exceeds the norm many times over, including kindergarten playgrounds. An independent group of doctors, having examined the children's thyroid glands, found not a single healthy child. Food is contaminated and you hear frightening rumors about the water. I learned all this at a meeting of a new organization, the Women's Society of Rukh, where a woman from the Geology Institute spoke— she herself made the chart. (I also spoke about Western feminism, but what is my emancipation compared with the apocalypse that everyone thinks is imminent?) People, especially women with children, are simply in a panic. On the 15th, the day of the opening session of the Ukrainian Supreme Rada (Soviet),[9] the Women's Society of Rukh will begin a picket outside the Supreme Rada building, with slogans demanding that the question of Chernobyl be placed on the agenda. I don't know that it will help. The bureaucrats appear to believe that their party cards will save them even from radiation.

The Jews are leaving Kiev in ever greater numbers. It seems everyone wants to leave. My friend, a Ukrainian poet, bemoans the fact she isn't Jewish. A sample of the milk served at her son's day care center revealed an increased dosage of radiation. Another of my friends has sent a letter to the Australian embassy with a request for immigration. No one wants to live here. People look at me as though I were mad, asking me why I came back. They say, "*You* have the chance, so go!" But I look at my child and my heart aches. Not just figuratively, but literally, and every day. What will happen to her? In such conditions, thinking such thoughts, it's hard to dissemble and pretend that everything is normal.

The worst thing for me is that I don't have high hopes for Rukh (maybe because right now I'm in a pessimistic frame of mind). Rukh too is becoming a bureaucracy, and some of the people who work there behave very rudely. Same thing in the Ukrainian Language Society.[10] I reminded my father about sending a letter thanking the Brazilian MP for her work in introducing Ukrainian into the state schools in Parana. He says that nobody's doing anything in the executive of the Language Society; everybody wants to be in charge. The leaders, like the hetmans of old, don't concentrate on the matters at hand, but squabble about who is going to be the chiefest among them.

May 14

Today I walked across that same square on Khreshchatyk. The blue-and-yellow flag is no longer there. It seems that the militia, i.e., the police, arrived yesterday and drove everyone away. That is, those who left voluntarily they let go; those who didn't want to leave they took away.

Yesterday, in the city of Poltava and in Poltava oblast, there was a large-scale police action. The Union of Ukrainian Youth was celebrating Petliura's[11] birthday and the authorities reacted in corresponding fashion, holding people up at the bus and train stations so that as few as possible could get to Symon's party.

The General Council of the Language Society met on Saturday and passed a motion of protest to President Gorbachev about the implementation of the official language law on the territory of the USSR. Levko Lukianenko[12] showed up and made a statement, saying more or less the following: "There is no point in harping on the language question. The question that needs to be raised is that of an independent state. Join the Ukrainian Republican party!"[13] Some people laugh at the URP, which has adopted a centralized structure. At the meeting itself somebody got up to say that such centralization smacks of Bolshevism. This doesn't surprise me: people often fight totalitarianism with totalitarianism. Nonetheless, the meeting concluded successfully and nominated Levko Lukianenko as their candidate to head parliament. The Communist party has put forward Ivashko.[14]

A new party has been formed—the Democratic party of Ukraine. At a meeting of its organizing committee on Sunday, there were agonizing debates about the name: should it be the "People's party of Ukraine," or the "Ukrainian People's party," or the "Democratic party"? Badzio,[15] who has left the Ukrainian Helsinki Union,[16] wrote the program and manifesto. The same people who edited the Rukh program are editing this one, and the declaration will be published over their names.

There's a real revolution going on in Lviv, with live broadcasts of the oblast and city council meetings. At those sessions that Chornovil[17] chairs, everyone is referred to as "mister" and "madam." "Comrade" no longer exists. (It's the same in many other structures, such as the Women's Society of Rukh; it even goes on in the Kiev city council. In the streets of Kiev you can also hear this form of address.) But these are rituals. It's interesting that in Lviv they've decided to remove the Lenin monument and put a Shevchenko monument in its place. Perhaps you know the whole complicated story about a site for the Shevchenko Monument. They've been looking for one for years, and now, as you see, they've finally found one. In Kiev they're talking more and more loudly about closing the Lenin Museum, as though it were somehow inevitable. The problem really is what to do with it—turn it into an art gallery, a children's center, or some sort of deputies' club.

One more event today. A small group—the Committee in Solidarity with Lithuania—is picketing city council. Such committees are active. There is also a Lithuanian Club. There are all kinds of posters around Kiev in support of Lithuania.

Yesterday on central television Borys Oliinyk made an appearance on the main news broadcast. There had been some kind of deliberations about Russia at the All-Union Cultural Fund. The Russian people, he proclaimed, are "mighty" and "great" and have need of only one thing: to be Russian. So Russians have to be more Russian. No comment required.

But tomorrow is the most interesting of all. Tomorrow our Parliament begins its work.

May 15

From the morning on there are pickets, delegations from the oblasts, and all kinds of slogans hoisted in the square near the Supreme Rada. Some are ecological, while the political ones for the most part argue the necessity of a free Ukraine. There are many slogans against the former head of the Supreme Rada, Valentyna Shevchenko, and those against Ivashko and Masol, the head of the Council of Ministers. The crowd is restless, greeting deputies of various stripes with insulting catcalls and applauding others. So one of the major questions of this first day is how to react to this. Artemenko, a deputy from Luhansk oblast, suggested that the crowd be dispersed. This provoked a storm of protest from the Democratic Bloc.[18] The crowd is demanding live audio transmission into the square, but the session voted in a majority against this.

The question of television and radio broadcast of the sessions took up a great deal of time. The apparatus had decided beforehand to provide an abbreviated version. The deputies, however, began the session with a proposal (from my father) that all sessions be broadcast live. In the end, Leonid Kravchuk's[19] proposal was accepted: to broadcast directly by radio and after six o'clock on television.

In the elections to the temporary presidium of parliament, none from the Democratic Bloc got in, the majority having pushed their own people through. More than 200 even voted against Salii, the reform-minded boss of the party organization in Kiev's Podil district. Pliushch,[20] the chairman of the Kiev oblast council, is not as blatant as Lukianov, who heads parliament in Moscow, but speaks a frightful *surzhyk* (mixture of Russian and Ukrainian). My ears can hardly stand it. In spite of the electronic technology, the microphones placed in front of each deputy aren't working. Representatives from the old presidium said they didn't have time to carry out the technical preparations properly. Didn't have time?

The Democratic Bloc is demanding that the question of the report from the previous Supreme Rada (i.e., Valentyna Shevchenko's report) be put on the agenda, as well as the Chernobyl question. The "right" is resisting.

May 18

The day before yesterday, on the 16th, the deputies discussed various procedural questions, beginning with the "standing strike" of deputies from the Democratic Bloc, who announced that they would remain standing until the loud-speakers for direct broadcast into the square were turned on. They stood while the question was once more put to the vote, and finally the loudspeakers were turned on. The effect is stunning, even on t.v. Next they discussed the Petliura birthday commemoration in Poltava (the minister of internal affairs, Hladush, gave an explanation, and in the evening in the square before the Supreme Rada a crowd yelled out in unison, "Shame on Hladush!"). They also elected the mandate commission after a long struggle (some of those who managed to get on have official complaints against them). The Metropolitan of Vinnytsia or Rivne (I don't remember exactly) scandalized everyone when he referred to the Ukrainian Catholic church as "so-called." The Galicians protested. The Lviv writer Roman Ivanychuk made an impassioned speech.

But the most important business was the drawing up of the agenda. There had been demands that the questions of Chernobyl and the report of the government be added; the newly created agrarian group demanded that the question of the prioritized development of villages be added. Some of the speeches were extraordinary. For example, Altunian,[21] an Armenian from Kharkiv, spoke eloquently about the suppression of the blue-and-yellow flag, and so on. An agrarian from Kharkiv spoke in *surzhyk* about the servitude of the villages and how they are being destroyed. The newspapers, by the way, do not publish these presentations.

Yesterday, the 17th, Chairman Pliushch lost his cool to the point that he drove even Kravchuk from the podium. The atmosphere is becoming ever more strained and unstable. The confirmation of the deputies' mandates, carried out in spite of electors' complaints and violations in certain constituencies, is a scandal.[22] Pavlo Movchan made a speech about this, to no avail.

A vote was held on the agenda. Then Ukraine's sovereignty was endorsed by a majority. Everyone has his or her idea of what sovereignty is—even the CPSU is for it. Speaking to this, Dmytro Pavlychko said that we're all for the independence of Ukraine—we only have to agree how to achieve it. Everything proceeded normally. Meanwhile, in the square, the majority of slogans was against the CPSU.

Nevertheless, the day ended in scandal. The day before yesterday, Chornovil had proposed that the public be given the telephone numbers to parliament's secretariat so they can phone in their views. Yesterday secretariat member Stadnychenko read out a brief about the issues addressed by telephone callers. And, naturally, most of the public is indignant about the Democratic Bloc. So it is alleged. When there was criticism of Larysa Skoryk, allegedly from the electorate, everyone in the hall leapt from his place and threw himself at the podium. The "right" did so as well, understanding as they did that such "evidence by telephone" could be gathered against them too. An uproar ensued, very nearly a scuffle; the radio transmission was shut down; and on t.v. they substituted cheery music. Such is our parliament.

May 19

The next day, the head of the secretariat apologized for Stadnychenko. But as far as the public was concerned, Stadnychenko, editor of *Radianska Ukraina* (Soviet Ukraine, the Communist party newspaper), had shown his true colors. Yesterday parliament finally drew up the agenda, a big job, and confirmed the rules of order. Masol's report is on the agenda. I'll bet that, after he presents it, his chances of being elected chairman of the Council of Ministers will not be great. Tension has abated somewhat, although scandalous situations are breaking out everywhere. One day Porovsky, a deputy from the Democratic Bloc, proposed removing the statue of Lenin from parliament's chambers, which raised a storm of protest. Another democrat, Serhii Holovaty, commented to the Kiev Komsomol newspaper *Moloda Hvardiia* (Young Guard) that he supported the idea, for there should be no political insignia in the hall except the flag.

There are little blue-and-yellow flags on stands in front of a few deputies from the Democratic Bloc. There are many who wear two badges on their lapels—the official blue-and-red deputy's banner and the national blue-and-yellow one. Some wear embroidered shirts. In his sky-blue embroidered shirt and with his Cossack mustache, Levko Lukianenko wanders about the hall, looking like Taras Shevchenko himself.

Yesterday at our institute there was a meeting to hear the report of the party committee members. The majority was taken aback when a few announced their resignations from the CPSU, Slava Briukhovetsky and I among them. Of the 82 communists in our institute, six have now withdrawn.

Elected to the Academy were Zatonsky and Oliinyk. D[mytro] P[avlychko] didn't make it. Neither did Dziuba, but they elected Zhulynsky corresponding member. As Briukhovetsky said to us at the institute meeting yesterday, "They made Oliinyk an academician as a reward for his betrayal of Rukh." But the rumor is going the rounds that Oliinyk didn't make it as a delegate to the CPSU congress from his own native Poltava district. There is still no official confirmation of the results of the elections to the party congress. They took place on the 17th.

May 22

More about our Kievan political battles. On Sunday, the 19th, the Democratic Bloc held a meeting, the principal agenda

item of which was the candidacy for the chairmanship of the
Supreme Rada. At previous meetings, the names of Drach,[23]
Dmytro Pavlychko, Levko Lukianenko from the Ukrainian
Republican party, and Mykhailo Horyn[24] had all been mentioned. On Sunday, after some wrangling, the bloc agreed to
nominate a single candidate, Academician Yukhnovsky.[25]
Chornovil was very anxious to go up against Ivashko and then
to propose that both their candidacies be withdrawn. But since
the opposition has no chance of winning this post, the basic
question is how to deal with Ivashko's candidacy.

Yesterday, the 20th, the parliamentary session once again
erupted in scandal. The "right" unexpectedly made a proposal
to carry the official Soviet Ukrainian flag into the hall. (Someone from the party Central Committee must have been ponder-
ing all weekend about the best way to annoy the democrats.)
This proposal came from the Luhansk delegation. The Democratic Bloc took it as a provocation and its members left the
hall to caucus. When they returned to the highly agitated
discussion, it was suggested that two flags, state and national,
be put up, but this did not get through either. Then they
accepted Holovaty's proposal that no flags be brought in; that
the democrats take down the blue-and-yellow ones from their
stands; and that the question be taken up again during the
discussion on Ukrainian sovereignty.

The "right" is very jumpy. The democrats represent only
a third, but they are always at the microphones and dominate
the hall as if they constituted a majority.

There followed a discussion of rules of order, including an
important point about the requirement of a minimum of two
candidates in the election of the chairman of the Supreme
Rada. In the rules of order, practically every word is put to a
vote, and the "right" blocks almost every proposal made by
the democrats.

Each day ends with a very interesting hour allotted to
miscellaneous items. Yesterday a representative of the "Independence" group, a formation comprising 21 deputies, announced (in Russian!) that they had invited a representative of
the Lithuanian parliament and asked that he be allowed to

speak. Chairman Pliushch was visibly shocked and surprised, but the pressure was so great that he had to give the Lithuanian the floor. He spoke for about two minutes, reading out (in the Ukrainian language!) greetings to the Parliament and the people of Ukraine in the name of Lithuania, signed by Landsbergis, and then informed us that Lithuania was proposing to take 5,000 children from the Chernobyl zone for the summer as of June 1. The man is in fact the head of the Lithuanian parliamentary committee on Chernobyl. I imagine that this proposal and his speech may elicit a great response from the public, which is very disturbed by all Chernobyl-related topics. One more interesting question. The Ternopil oblast council has refused the Ministry of Defense some land for a firing range. Or, rather, they've decided to create a park where the range now stands. The army, naturally, has no intention of leaving. So now the oblast council is appealing to the Supreme Rada to "rescind the occupation policies of the military." Kravchuk intervened with a fiery eulogy of Lenin, saying that this historical figure was undoubtedly a genius and to criticize him is shameful. Levko Lukianenko replied, presenting his own thoughts. You can imagine what they were.

May 23

There was a significant event yesterday—a meeting near the Shevchenko monument to commemorate the transfer of his remains to Ukraine. First thing, at the morning session, Drach, the head of Rukh, proposed to the deputies that they lay wreaths at the monument. Together with Pliushch, he laid the first wreath at 7:00 p.m. A crowd had already gathered at the monument, bearing dozens of blue-and-yellow flags, and even two red-and-black Banderist ones. (Banderism[26] is making a formidable comeback, which terrifies me. I have an elegant red-and-black French umbrella that I'm already afraid to carry in the street. Recently, when I was carrying it on Kirov Street near my institute, two young men shouted a Banderist slogan at me. Can you imagine? In the center of Kiev! I've noticed that a large number of people have begun to wear red-and-black badges.)

Another large crowd arrived from the parliament square with deputies Oles Shevchenko and Levko Lukianenko, both former political prisoners, at their head. The women and children wore outfits exclusively of blue and yellow colors, and crosses around their necks. (The women's long plush skirts gave the whole thing the air of an operetta.) I think this was an Autocephalous Orthodox[27] group. The Autocephalous priest, who was quite hoarse, led a brief service, while a deputy bishop of the Russian Orthodox[28] church who was also a parliamentary deputy stood around for a short time and then left. A child read the Lord's Prayer. Still other, unknown people recited religious and patriotic verses of poor literary quality, but the crowd roared its approval nevertheless and got all choked up. This religious frenzy rather saddened me. It's unsettling even to think that the small boy who stood for several hours on the steps to the monument, holding a cross and wearing yellow Cossack pants, may somehow be identified with the future of Ukraine.

The main slogan of the meeting was "Glory to Ukraine!" They shouted it out three times in a row, with three fingers held up, symbolizing the national emblem—the trident. Some former dissidents, now deputies, elbowed aside the writers who had prepared their own program, but later the writers managed to shove their way through to the monument. Mushketyk, the head of the Writers' Union, spoke. Then our Harvard friend Grabowicz, who also concluded with the words "Glory to Ukraine; then the affable Rutgers professor Hunczak and Hawrylyshyn from the Geneva International Management Institute; the poet Moisei Fishbein, from Israel; then Drach, Pavlychko, and Chornovil; then Zhdankin sang a song of the Ukrainian Sich Riflemen. The theme of all the speeches was independence. This word is now on everyone's lips, not just in their thoughts. Some of the slogans were a little peculiar, e.g., borrowing from Shevchenko, "Ukraine has fought to the end. The communists torture her even more savagely than the Polish nobles." One of the placards, there was a real sock full of holes (a work of home-made pop art) and the words (in Russian), "Under the communists we were without socks; soon we'll be going around without pants."

Because of the meeting, I missed half the broadcast of the parliamentary session, where there was another scandal. Chornovil had clumsily opined that the former Supreme Rada had harbored "swineherds and milkmaids" [party mouthpieces]; the "right" jumped up in protest from their seats, as they had learned to do from the Democratic Bloc. It's true that Pliushch quashed the uproar, not even giving the floor to Ivashko, who had flung himself toward the podium. Yesterday, at long last, temporary "rules of order" were adopted. Now more interesting things can begin.

Holovaty made a comical announcement about the "right's" blocking of each of the Democratic Bloc's proposals. He said that should the right decide he was wearing a white suit, and the Democratic Bloc decide he was in black, parliament would vote that Holovaty was wearing a white suit. In fact, he was wearing black. At this, Pliushch waved him off.

May 24

Yesterday once again I missed a large part of the television broadcast of parliamentary debates because the Women's Society of Rukh was meeting. I have some hopes for this group. For now, its main concern is ecological. A report has been issued with some terrifying data about the consequences of Chernobyl. Thirty-two districts of Ukraine are polluted with radioactive fallout, and there is a huge number of hot spots in Kiev. They decided to publish these materials under the aegis of the Women's Society and distribute them around Kiev. On the day that parliament was to consider the Chernobyl question, they again organized pickets and signed a petition with demands to the Supreme Rada. On the whole, the mood of the meeting was somber. The largest part of the radiation has settled at the bottom of the Kiev reservoir, which means that a flood could stir it up and carry it off to the Dnieper, poisoning the whole of southern Ukraine. What shocks me most of all is that even today far too many people live with the stupid Ukrainian conviction that "somehow things will work out." This is particularly true of men. I took Oksana and George Grabowicz to the meeting. When we dropped in at the Writers' Union, "men" (i.e., "writers") were coming out. They regarded Grabowicz with great suspicion. What's *he* doing, going to a women's organization? It is my opinion that not even a thousand years will be enough to transform the culture of the Ukrainian male. Not even a sovereign Ukraine will help.

Yesterday at the parliamentary session they spent the whole day discussing the agenda, debating the question of the priority of discussion items. Again, it was from the farthest right that a motion was made to elect the chairman of the Supreme Rada first, then proceed to the report of the previous government. Some said no report was necessary. You can go into any shop, see the empty shelves, and that would be the entire report. The Democratic Bloc again protested this obvious manipulation by the secretariat and the "right." But this was an unexpected move even for Ivashko, who suggested that the report be heard first. In the session's secretariat, it appears, there are forces that don't much care for Ivashko. Clearly, Ivashko is playing at being a democrat. He even goes about on foot or is chauffeured around in a Zhiguli (Lada) instead of using his predecessor's black Zil limousine. Moreover, Ivashko said that it was necessary to proceed as quickly as possible to the question of sovereignty. Yeltsin is said to have announced that Russia will start selling Ukraine oil for dollars. As incredible as it seems, there are those in Russia who want to separate. Good riddance.

May 25

At yesterday's session Masol read his report for one hour and twenty minutes. Absurdly, Masol is full of optimism. His cabinet has been in power for two and one-half years; he announced that in another two years the economy would be

righted. This only irritates people, of course. He skirted around
the political situation, saying only that sovereignty is necessary;
that Moscow is grabbing everything (earlier, only 7% of
industry was under republican control; now it's 40%) and so
on.

947
. 781

There followed two hours of discussion about how to
discuss the report. The chairman suggested that representatives
from each oblast speak, followed by the representatives of
factions. The Democratic Bloc became nervous, as proceeding
by oblast would diminish its members' participation. They
finally agreed that there would be two lists of speakers—one
from the oblasts and another from the register of speakers
drawn up the day before, according to the rules of order. And
the Democratic Bloc predominates on that list.

What a surprise we got when the deputies began to speak.
It appears that no one from the oblasts supports government
policy! With the exception of one speaker from the Crimea, all
condemned the report and the work of the government, and
did not mince words either. Secretaries of regional committees
and oblasts spoke, as did directors of factories and enterprises,
and, in a very sound, competent and sage manner, analyzed
and exposed the administrative system that Masol and his
government are striving to cover up; the notion of the "regulated market" that originated in Moscow; the plunder of the
oblasts; the simply idiotic decrees concerning fixed prices for
grain, also adopted in Moscow; the ecological situation.... You
can't even keep track of all the criticism. But for the first time
in all the days of their deliberations, I was left feeling more
optimistic. Gorbachev got some of it too, as did some of his
aides, the "obscurantist" economists, as someone expressed it.
The co-operator from Dnipropetrovsk, Taburiansky,[29] was
especially well-spoken.

Altunian from Kharkiv stunned everybody, saying he
regretted that it was not possible to organize a faction of
former political prisoners. According to the rules, you need a
minimum of twenty people for this, and there are only about
ten of them in the Supreme Rada. He spoke about only one
thing—the necessity of putting the KGB under control,

publicizing its budget, closing down the regional and oblast committees, and making restitution to the former prisoners for their moral and material losses. The speech was emotional, even shocking to many, but was received with applause.

Panic reigns beyond the walls of the Supreme Soviet. A deputy from Dnipropetrovsk said that shops there have only salt and matches left for sale. Two days ago, Prime Minister Ryzhkov made an appearance on t.v. and announced a price hike. But this is an unparalleled absurdity. If we are to have a market economy, where does he—and his fixed, uniform prices for the whole monster from the Carpathian Mountains to Vladivostok—come in?

May 26

Yesterday the parliamentary debates on Masol's report continued in the same constructive spirit. The "right" is evolving leftward and criticizing the government. One speaker from Cherkasy—in an embroidered shirt, no less—thanked the government, but this was exceptional. There is an ever stronger whiff of sovereignty. From "our" side, Yavorivsky spoke well, Larysa Skoryk and Zaiets not so well. The representative from Ivano-Frankivsk was also very good.

There were elections in Russia yesterday. Yeltsin received a plurality of votes, but not the number required. His program is the separation and independence of Russia. Once again we look upon Moscow with trepidation. If Yeltsin should come to power, something interesting is bound to happen.

There was yet another incident involving Lenin. Deputy Stepan Khmara had only just begun to criticize Lenin in his speech when the communists jumped up and drove him from the podium. Actually, Khmara hadn't said anything particularly shocking, but he chose an inopportune moment. This could tell against the Democratic Bloc when parliament turns to electing members of the cabinet. Endless consultations and "secret negotiations" are going on over the issue of the cabinet's composition. At any moment documents of a new party will be presented—first it was to be called democratic, then "people's" (*narodna*), then once again democratic. Konev stated with great conviction that he would never become a member of a "people's" party.

June 2

Yet one more political week has come to an end, the week of the nomination of candidates to the chairmanship of the Supreme Rada. Ten men were in the running: Ivashko, Salii, Hryniov, Yukhnovsky, Horyn, Chornovil, Lukianenko, Drach, Pavlychko and Yavorivsky. They all outlined their programs and answered questions. (I won't write about that. It's all in *Radianska Ukraina*.) Everyone listened in, all of Ukraine sitting by its television set. The "right" said this was all a show; that the podium had been exploited for the airing of political declarations. They weren't far off the mark, of course. The last seven on the list didn't have a chance, but they all got the floor. And all, except Yukhnovsky, were for leaving the USSR. Yukhnovsky, in my opinion, is playing a political game. He attracted some support from outside the Democratic Bloc and disillusioned others with his "centrism." So, for two days, the words "separation" and "independence" rang in the air, and ring still, as a kind of cliché. Some of the speeches during the debate turned out to be interesting. First of all, they smeared three writers who were candidates, digging up all the old citations in praise of Moscow and the Communist party, and read them out, insinuating Petliurism and Banderism. Drach threatened to take one of the speakers to court. From the left, there were fine, and not so fine, speeches. The main line was a critique of the Communist party and accordingly of Ivashko. In this respect, Holovaty spoke particularly well and Konev was fantastic when he made an appeal not to take part in the new government or bend to any compromise.

Four candidates remained in the running: Ivashko, Hryniov, Salii and Yukhnovsky. The elections will take place two days from now, on Monday. I think that Ivashko will win, but, as for what happens after that, nothing is clear. It's hard to predict developments; people are nervous and aggressive. A throng stands outside the Supreme Rada and shouts, "Ivashko's gotta go!" The situation is nearly explosive. We are living on top of a powder keg. The main political question is: are we in a pre- or post-revolutionary situation? Moldavia is the first state to have recognized Lithuania. Yeltsin has also announced his intention to establish direct contacts with Lithuania. At Yeltsin's press conference, someone referred to the Supreme Soviet of the USSR as a House of Lords that won't be deciding anything one of these days, and compared Gorbachev to the Queen of England. I think that the USSR Supreme Soviet may not even complete its term. And it's almost certain that the Ryzhkov government will collapse. More and more often you hear calls for the dismissal of this government.

Kiev is full of foreign journalists. Yesterday I met for an hour with correspondents from West Germany who came to the Women's Society of Rukh, and today BBC correspondents came to my home. In Canada (and wasn't it thanks to your gentle direction?) I learned how to give interviews, and this knack comes in handy here. But politics is very wearying and debilitating, even for someone who is just an observer. It acts like a narcotic, though. I'm continuing to collect newspapers for you, but nobody wants to take them to Canada.

There is a good chance that our feminist anthology will appear next year. At the moment, I'm most concerned about the quality of the essays and the reliability of the authors.

June 15

Our political passions have cooled somewhat with the election of the head of the Supreme Rada and two deputy chairmen and with the emergence of the Narodna Rada (People's Council), which is to say of the opposition (formerly called the Democratic Bloc), under the leadership of Yukhnov-sky. Parliament has been on the edge of political crisis a few times. It took a very long time to decide on the names of the standing commissions, and in secret negotiations with the chairman the opposition managed to wrest a third of the commission chairs for itself. I'm sure Dmytro Pavlychko, while in Canada, will tell you all about this in detail. He knows all the twists and turns of the game. The Narodna Rada is barely organized and hard to manage. Mr. Khmara, for example, announced that he will not make the least compromise and accused Yukhnovsky of collaborating with an anti-national regime. Something in that spirit. He is joined by a couple more people who refuse to vote. But people have generally cooled off. This session of parliament has taken only one decision in a month—to go from Moscow to local, that is, Kiev time.

All eyes are fixed on Moscow, where Yeltsin is making history. Independence and the collapse of our last empire cannot be far off: there are forecasts that the USSR Supreme Soviet, to which Oliinyk is a deputy, will not last more than two months. A Ukrainian Soccer Federation is to be created this autumn; there will be a Ukrainian championship, and so on. Thus, we are separating by degrees. We await the Communist party congress in Moscow. We hope it's the last. A split in the CPSU is imminent, as almost everyone now openly acknowledges. A party conference opens in Moscow on June 19 to establish a Russian Communist party. It looks like a Politburo ruse to neutralize Yeltsin and the Russian parliament.

I have dozens of things to do—I'm finishing a book about the British novel of ideas, but my head is wrapped up entirely in feminist theory. I've gathered together a small group of women scholars and we are studying the literature that I brought back (unfortunately, not very much). We discuss feminist theory as it applies to our problems. I myself plan to write an article, "Is Feminism Necessary in Ukraine?" and perhaps something longer. The opposition to feminism is frightful. We don't exactly broadcast notice of our meetings, but we don't hide them either; a number of my male colleagues and even some women betray nervousness, or even scorn. The same goes for the Women's Society of Rukh. There is, as usual, other, even titillating, news. It seems that perestroika has even begun to penetrate our Academy. But we'll talk about all this in England.

In the meantime, read our Ukrainian samizdat. It's true that some of it is rubbish, for example, the broadsheet of the Ukrainian National party (i.e., primitive nationalists, very similar to your Banderists). The official newspapers are often markedly more interesting. The best Soviet newspaper now is *Kommersant* (Businessman), the organ of the Union of Co-operatives, which is published in Moscow.

June 22

I've been feeling quite fed up with these letters of mine, but I've somehow pulled myself together and so I continue, thanks to the computer.

Today is Friday. Parliament is in recess until Monday. All the same, there have been some interesting events this week. In fact, they occur daily and several at once.

On Tuesday the Russian Communist party conference opened in Moscow. This is a special and not altogether clear story. Only a couple of months ago the leadership of the CPSU wouldn't hear of a separate Russian party organization, and so it began as an underground initiative. Its constituent conference took place in Leningrad two months ago. It was a convention of such conservatives that even the First Secretary of the Leningrad oblast committee, Gidaspov, one of the party's most hard-core conservatives, didn't want to have anything to do with them. But when Yeltsin came to power in the Russian parliament, everything changed, and the party's official leadership is now going full steam ahead on creating a Russian Communist party.

On the second day, the conference, under the chairmanship of Gorbachev, made the decision to confer on itself the status of a founding conference. Nominations for First Secretary were held yesterday, among the candidates is the "darling of the party," Ivan Polozkov, First Secretary of the Krasnodar oblast committee, who failed in his bid as chairman of the

RSFSR Supreme Soviet. Recently, the notorious Nina Andreeva, conservative of conservatives, sang his praises in *Argumenty i Fakty*. In discussions about his candidacy, it was said of him that he wouldn't be able to consolidate the party. (What does this mean, "to consolidate" it? It's a popular term these days, especially on the lips of the "partocracy," but it doesn't make any sense.) Nevertheless, he's the most likely candidate, if you consider the composition of this congress.

The conference, and now the congress, demonstrate how quickly the CPSU is moving to the right. Representatives of other platforms and party factions with their programs also participated. The Marxist—or, rather, Bolshevik—program is sheer populism, demagogy, sloganeering—everything for the workers, in theory; everything on their behalf, while they, the workers, are leaving the party in droves. The rich to be punished. In a word, for the dictatorship of the proletariat.

The platform of the Leningrad constituent conference of the Russian CP, with its undisguised chauvinism, is even more right-wing. Their representative said, in so many words, "We aren't going to be liked by those who haven't the guts to hear two words: Russian and Communist." They applauded him. There's something about it that gives me the creeps. And not only me. In Kiev, people express real fear when talking about this Russian CP congress. People are afraid of a union of Pamiat, Gidaspov, Ligachev, all the right-wingers, and all the generals, even of a fascist coup. The term "fascist" is not mine—I've already heard it spoken several times. However, while the party moves to the right, the rank and file is deserting it.

Everywhere there is talk of the threat of a right-wing coup. A possible variation involves the coup leaders' adoption of certain economic reforms, just to toss a bone to the people. This very idea was expressed by a well-known economist. And when I said I doubted any such possibility, he said it was possible as a kind of experiment. This wouldn't be the first experiment in our state. Moreover, there is the example of China.

The democratic platform at the Russian party conference

leaves a better impression. But even the democrats are for a single CPSU and an undivided USSR. I think that the democratic platform is another machination dreamed up at the top. Few of its adherents are at the congress, even though it's reckoned that 40% of all communists support the platform. The delegates criticize Gorbachev, but often this criticism comes from the right. It appears that the rightists would like to heap the blame on him for the failures of perestroika, and to get rid of him.

The Communist Party of Ukraine (CPU) congress is going on in Kiev, and it's the same thing here. Nothing but incantations of loyalty to ideals. Incantations and ritual anthems. Criticisms of the Politburo of the CPU, also often from the right. They complain that the communists are not working well in parliament; that they've relinquished the ideological commissions to the opposition. At the same time, they abuse the writers on all sides, especially the "renegade former communists." Everyone is talking about the crisis in the Communist party and its loss of authority. But the consolidation that the speakers are on about would have to happen on completely unacceptable and conservative terms—the CPU as part of the CPSU; a new Union treaty. The public is not following this congress with any great attention. For them it's clear who will be elected and what resolutions will be adopted.

June 24

Two party forums completed their business yesterday. In Moscow, they've elected Polozkov; in Kiev, Hurenko, just as everyone expected. Salii, the secretary of the Kiev regional committee, who represented the reform current, ran as an opponent to Hurenko. Other candidates withdrew, among them even the "Afghan" general, Gromov. There's a party leader for you! He had enough sense to withdraw his candidacy, but the very fact that it was put forward speaks volumes. Salii's candidacy was wrecked, of course. On top of that, they cursed him roundly. Even *Radianska Ukraina* noted that it is unseemly to drag your opponent through the mud, as if at an open meeting. Of course, Salii is not a leader of the same caliber as Yeltsin. He doesn't command much authority.

Leonid Kravchuk has become the second secretary of the Central Committee. Kukhar, vice-president of the Academy of Sciences of the Ukrainian SSR, has also joined the Politburo. Probably he'll take Paton's place as president of the Academy. The party's upper echelons are made up of true "Leninists" who unanimously vilified Rukh not long ago. There are new people in the Politburo: workers. Obviously they're there so everyone can see that the CPU is the party of the working class. You can't sense any leftward movement in the CPU; on the contrary, everything is gearing up for a big battle. It is impossible to foresee the future.

At the same time, the "oppositionists" had their meeting. (I sat through a day at Rukh's Grand Council.) It took place in what is now the Teachers' Building, where the Central Rada[30] proclaimed the First Universal.

In very large measure this was a historic meeting, the first since the elections, in which Rukh candidates were elected as deputies at all levels and in some regions even won a majority of seats. Ivan Drach conducted the meeting. Yavorivsky, Cherniak, Konev and Mykhailo Horyn sat next to him in the Presidium.

In his report, entitled "The Political Situation in Ukraine and Rukh's Tasks," Drach included, as always, many literary metaphors and historical parallels. The main political news was the development of an opposition within the opposition—i.e., the advent of a radical faction in the Narodna Rada. Drach said that the next opposition to the opposition will have a platform similar to that of Ivashko himself. Later this phrasing brought the criticism of the "ultra-radicals" down on Drach's head. Drach made an appeal to pluralism. Exactly a week ago at Rukh's public assembly in Kiev there were calls for the expulsion of all communists from the meeting hall.

Drach reiterated his old theme of public apathy. If 100,000 people had gathered at the Supreme Rada on the day the head of parliament was elected, instead of 4,000, Ivashko would not have won. This, of course, is to the point, and very sad. Our regime has destroyed the most important thing in a person: initiative, life itself. The brutalization, demoralization and moral apathy of people are unbelievable. People in the streets are sullen and preoccupied. They're preoccupied for the most part with just eking out a living by managing to get some kind of food, some kind of clothing, in order to live through yet another day, to save their kids from radiation, or simply to survive.

The most painful point in Drach's report—and in the thoughts of the leading personalities of Ukraine—is the situation in Russia. Half a year ago, Yeltsin said that he wants complete sovereignty for Russia. Today, in the RSFSR Declaration of Sovereignty, we read, "within the borders of the Union." In essence, the chief question of Drach's report is whether a Union treaty is necessary. And the clear answer is that it is unnecessary. In this we may discern Rukh's new strategy, its new program. And that is the struggle for Ukraine's withdrawal from the Union. That which earlier had been declared only within the Ukrainian Helsinki Group has become the general view, as all the subsequent reports and presentations attested.

The next speaker was the economist Oleksandr Savchenko.[31] His theme was how Ukraine may overcome the economic crisis. His main idea was that political independence must precede economic sovereignty, if only by half a step. The economic variant of the Ryzhkov-Gorbachev reform (the notion of a "limited" or "regulated" market) exists only to deceive the West, to wheedle investments. If the USSR is preserved, the market becomes a perilous factor, because there would be a single labor and housing market. From this arises the danger, for instance, that rich Siberians will buy up Ukraine, grab all the apartments, and so on.

The next point is that if the Union is now going to be taking loans from Western corporations, then they will be watching to see that the Union hangs together. For who will repay the debts after the collapse of the USSR?

Savchenko proposed a Declaration of Sovereignty (he

didn't stress what kind of sovereignty, but obviously meant complete withdrawal) and a refusal to pay taxes to the Union. He would use the money to finance our own Ministry of Internal Affairs and KGB and all the rest, and to raise salaries. Today this could still be carried out without lowering the standard of living; a year from now, the Polish model awaits us.

Perhaps it's so (I think to myself), but can one today realistically refuse to pay taxes to the Union treasury? Who would do it? Our Supreme Rada? That's utopian. Ivashko's parliament would never do it. Does another trap lie in wait for us?

The next to speak was Serhii Konev—thin and temperamental. He spoke about the prospects for Rukh's activities and proposed a conference[32] of the democratic city and oblast radas (soviets) of Ukraine in Dniprodzerzhynsk. This is an initiative of the Dniprodzerzhynsk council—to create an "eastern" branch of Rukh which would have its own specific agenda. Rukh is now undergoing a crisis: new parties will be forming on Rukh's foundations, and people will join them. Our task is not to let it wither away. Sociological research is necessary.

Ternopilsky spoke, in place of Holovaty, about amending the Rukh statutes. Rukh is already in need of reconstruction or expansion. A paradox—so soon!

Korbetsky (an impressive scholar from Kiev, who spoke in Russian) proposed the creation of a Political Council of Rukh to which all the parties of the bloc would send representatives. He spoke of Leonid Kravchuk's provocative suggestion to the Ukrainian Language Society that it take charge of the application of the language law, made in the full knowledge that the public has no use for those "in charge." Kravchuk put it about that Rukh is waging a war mainly for symbols. Rukh proponents became involved in a discussion with him, which created the impression that symbols are the main issue. Korbetsky noted that already people are using the Russian language less and less in meetings. Russians are leaving Rukh, which risks transforming Rukh into an exclusively Ukrainian movement.

Burakovsky, head of the Jewish association, spoke about the work of the Rukh Council of Nationalities and criticized the official Cultural Fund, whose policies have led to splits within ethnic minority communities.

The astronomer and Doctor of Science, Shulman, touched on a very painful problem, on which Slava Briukhovetsky then expanded. He said that if a provocateur had penetrated Rukh, he would have exclaimed: Out with the communists! Out with the writers, the scholars, the workers in law-enforcement agencies, out with...! As a result, only former political prisoners and the nationalist Organization of Ukrainian Youth would be left in Rukh.

Then Briukhovetsky expanded on this thesis and recalled that, at the first elections, several young people had spoken abusively about academicians, forcing them off the stage. And now there are practically no scholars in the hall.

Biletsky from Donetsk, the only one to address the hall as "Ladies and Gentlemen," spoke about the situation in the east. The provocative idea of Donetsk's separating from Ukraine and the formation of a Donetsk International Republic is circulating there. True, people are now leaving the CPU. In 1989, 1,000 people left; in the first five months of 1990, another 1,000. (In his report, Ivashko said that 28,000 had left the CPU. I'm positive it's more. Statistics here are well hidden.) There are Rukh circles in all the towns of Donetsk now and the approval rating of Rukh activists is twice as high as that of party activists. The main problem is the lack of cadres, the ambitions of certain people, and mutual recriminations of insufficient radicalism. There are difficulties attendant on people's entering new parties. He also called for a reorientation toward the east. On the whole, easterners have shown real distinction in the Great Council. At the end, he called for targeting the extraordinary parliamentary elections two years from now.

Then, as usual in an orange embroidered shirt and with an inscrutable expression, Porovsky made an announcement. They say he's a good organizer, but very rough in manner and violent in appearance. He seems always on the point of unsheathing a Cossack sword.

Cherniak, a member of the USSR Congress of People's Deputies, spoke after the break. He wrote Rukh's economic program and now criticized Rukh most sharply, speaking against the intolerance that reigns there; about the need to engage professionally in politics. He said that parliament is not viable because it was formed in undemocratic conditions, and condemned the actions of the democratic bloc. In his view, the number one question is that of Rukh and its deputies, and he sees for Rukh only the role of a bloc of parties. Rukh today is going through a crisis. It has played out its historical role and can no longer continue as in the past. A new orientation is needed.

Taras Hunczak from New Jersey and Vasyl Kalymon from Toronto spoke for the diaspora, describing the activities of the Friends of Rukh (Kalymon) and assistance to the children of Chernobyl (Hunczak).

Samokhvalenko of Lutsk told us that as we spoke, a vigil was under way in Lutsk. On January 23, 1941, before the arrival of the Germans, the NKVD savagely executed prisoners held in several prisons of the region. In Lutsk today there's a human chain stretching from the regional KGB to the city jail. Historical injustice lies in the fact that the Germans then proceeded to shoot another 14,000 in Lutsk for alleged co-operation with the communists.

Larysa Skoryk's speech was symptomatic, revealing a serious crisis in the Narodna Rada of the Supreme Rada. She's a member of the radical faction in the opposition to which Drach referred. Rather sarcastically she criticized Drach and spoke about the objection of many to Yukhnovsky's compromise announcement on voting for the heads of commissions. (There had been an agreement with Ivashko: we'll vote for yours and you for ours.) After the incident with Hryniov (which came about because Hryniov wanted to conduct the meeting in Russian and even wanted to put this to a vote), six people left the Narodna Rada. Then the question arose with whom and to what extent to consolidate. There can be no consolidation with those for whom the language question is not a priority. Larysa is right about this. On the other hand, her position could be destructive. For the next step is a general exodus from parliament and partisan warfare. But politics is a subtle thing: many in the Narodna Rada, in my view, don't understand this, and impatiently shove aside the "inert masses." Skoryk was absolutely right about one thing: the Union treaty is dangerous and unnecessary.

After Skoryk, a young man, agitated as a little rooster, spoke on behalf of the Union of Student Youth. But when he said that Rukh had lost the elections, they started heckling him in the hall. People in Rukh, as in the CPU and in our government in general (another legacy of socialism), do not tolerate criticism. The orator pressed urgently for new elections and the takeover of power. Highly unrealistic.

Hubar, a professor from Cherkasy, said that our chief enemy is Bolshevism, that "hybrid of utopia and violence." He pressed for the market, saying that if there is a market, there will be no Bolshevism, for the two are incompatible. It sounds good, but it's not clear how we're to get there. He argued that Rukh should stay in opposition another two or three years, because it has no managerial cadre. Its current intellectual potential is insufficient.

A representative of the National Front of Belorussia spoke. In the Belorussian parliament the democrats also have a third of the seats, and the vice-president of the Supreme Soviet is also a democrat. Because there is a Ukrainian cultural center in Minsk, he called for the creation of a Belorussian cultural center in Kiev. This is correct. We must be made aware that it is only one-time Soviet republics that can understand one another. Even former dissidents in the Czech leadership have not recognized Lithuania—a stunning disappointment. Drach also spoke of this. Today in Belorussia the congress of the National-Democratic party opened. It too is for independence.

Levko Lukianenko spoke marvelously well. He commands a fantastic authority. Drach has said that he is our Mandela, only they welcome Mandela in America, but not Lukianenko; and, I would add, will never welcome him. Not long ago, the Lenin Prize committee, with Borys Paton newly at its head, awarded Mandela the Lenin Peace Prize, even though Sakharov had never received it. (For this move, the progressive press criticized the Lenin Prize committee.) And of course Levko Lukianenko has never even dreamed of it. The insincerity of our government is on display in living color. To shower a foreign dissident with favors and to crush one of our own at the same time!

In the Supreme Rada, along with Lukianenko, the current leader of the Ukrainian Republican party, there are twelve men from the Ukrainian Helsinki Union. He notes with justice that the political center is shifting from the streets to the Supreme Rada. And at this time Rukh is in the grip of a crisis. The main question is how to get out of it. Levko's answer is to go to the people. This goal has two variations: either activation of the masses to demand the recall of the conservative deputies in parliament, or undergoing a parliamentary crisis and new elections. The second way is the more dangerous one. It seems that, unlike many "radicals," Levko understands the extent of public apathy. It's my hypothesis that the public simply may not turn out for the next elections. Why should they, when nothing is changing for the better?

Lukianenko told us of his own "walkabout" among the people this week. He was in Vinnytsia, Berestechko, Rivne, and Chernihiv, where about 2,000 people showed up for a meeting. He called for participation in the celebration of 500 years of Cossackdom at the beginning of August. This festival is meant to inspire and revolutionize people. The organizers are counting on it.

Then a speaker from Dnipropetrovsk informed us that, at the time of the prison disturbances (recently there was a whole week of rioting in the Dnipropetrovsk interrogation "isolator"), a blue-and-yellow flag flew over the jail. He considered this a provocation.

As a person close to the "center," Bazylevsky, a representative of the Ukrainian community in Moscow, said that "never before have we faced such a right-wing danger as now." He made a request to raise the question of Ukrainian citizenship.

After that, the deputy Chervonii, a member of the

Ukrainian Helsinki Union, criticized Drach rather severely for insufficient radicalism. They say that Chervonii never smiles. He's very grave, young, elegant, and radical. As I understand it, he's from the "radical faction." But at this point I left the hall because I had to head home.

Discussion continued the next day. They decided to augment the statutes, to prepare for the next congress and for the 500th anniversary celebrations of Cossackdom in Zaporizhzhia, which are to take place in August. There was to be a big meeting at five o'clock. In the end the meeting wasn't so big: the era of meetings, it seems, has already passed.

Although everybody was talking about the crisis in Rukh, I was much more satisfied by the session of the Great Council of Rukh than by many other such meetings in the past. There was no euphoria or frenzied applause or standing ovations after every speech, as at the founding congress, nor anthem-singing and solemn oaths. Only three flags in the hall, and nobody waved them about. It's true that the hall wasn't full, but I don't know whether this was a positive or negative thing. The security at the door was water-tight. The young men with "Rukh" armbands let no one in without an invitation or mandate.

An interesting note: when I told a relative who had come in for the day from a village in the Ivano-Frankivsk region about the debates on the reasons for the crisis situation in Rukh, she became frightened. "What will happen when the people, who believe only in Rukh, find out about this?" she complained. "It's better that they not learn of it." The typical reaction of a person raised in a totalitarian state.

June 25-26

After a break, the Supreme Rada is once again in session. Ivashko proposed revising the rules of order and adopting the Declaration of Sovereignty. The democratic bloc had expected this. Such a tactic reflected not so much a wish for Ukraine's freedom as heavy breathing from Moscow. Whence the pressure to adopt the declaration as quickly as possible and draw up a new Union treaty. The opposition was inclined to torpedo this business. Others also proposed examining the question of the two commission chairmen who still haven't been confirmed and of the appointment of the chairman of the Council of Ministers. They took a vote and Ivashko's proposal didn't make it. They put the question of sovereignty aside for a couple of days, but only for a couple of days.

They began discussing the candidate for the post of chairman of the Council of Ministers. The candidate was Masol, the current head and a man of the old guard. He was rather weak on the main points (Lithuania and private property), revealing himself as vague and conservative. Even many communists consider him incompetent. The result was defeat. His own people did him in—after all, the opposition represents only a third of the total.

On Tuesday, the 26th, Ivashko put forward the chairman of the State Planning Committee, Vitold Fokin, for this position. Fokin said his program accords with Masol's, and this alienated the opposition. As Fokin himself said, he hates the words "private property" as much as he does the word "Mister." Earlier, he was considered a radical, especially after his article in *Literaturna Ukraina* (Literary Ukraine). Half a year ago, his economic program appeared more radical than the Rukh program, which raised the ire of large sections of the communist bloc. Now it seems that, in important details (Lithuania, for example), he's with Gorbachev/Ryzhkov for a limited market. Fokin's downfall lay in his attempt to appease all camps. It's telling that, for eighteen years, he had worked for the State Planning Committee. While speaking, Fokin bloomed like a little flower; he was overflowing with happiness. They say that when Masol was defeated, there was rejoicing in Fokin's domain, the State Planning Committee. People there were sure of the victory of Fokin, who for some time had cleverly been courting the writers and Rukh, at that time still the opposition-in-waiting.

It's interesting that Yukhnovsky more or less supported Fokin. This was a political blunder in its own way. Yemets likewise was not unambiguously negative. He announced that the opposition had not rallied behind a single candidate. Evidently, they did not expect Fokin to lose and they were glad it wasn't Masol who won the position. Cherniak harshly criticized Fokin and his program. He said that Ukraine needs a government of national salvation. It's funny how people will call for the dismissal of this or that regional council or government when what's needed is the dismantling of the system. The main question is the replacement of economic authority, denationalization, decentralization, depoliticization, de-KGB-ization, and so on. Cherniak's speech was the best today.

June 28

You can imagine the general astonishment when, Fokin having fallen through, Ivashko, either in desperation or out of a certain cunning (probably the latter, in order to play on opposing views), proposed two candidates for the post of chairman of the Council of Ministers—Cherniak and Masol. In his program, Cherniak (who, apparently, was up all night writing; he was also late for the meeting, since he had to get in from the distant Kiev suburb of Teremky, where he lives, by public transport, as he doesn't have a government car) said that he did not expect to win, and then announced a very radical program of reforms. He spoke heatedly, growing more and more excited by his own plans. He looked very authoritative. The right didn't know which way to turn, but some later supported Cherniak in the debate, though they're not democrats by a long shot.

A scandal ensued. During the voting, someone cast a ballot for the absent deputy, Umanets. Among other things, he's the director of the Chernobyl nuclear power station. Even here there's a certain logic. Obviously, this was meant to be a vote for Masol, who was also in the running as a candidate. Quite a trick! So they annulled the results and authorized an investigation and a new vote. This second vote was declared invalid for lack of a quorum. In effect, the right-wing "majority" boycotted the vote, though it's not clear why. Ivashko had cut off the broadcast earlier, so democracy has finished for the day, and we await the development of events. It's all a step towards early elections.

They've just now announced on the radio that Masol has got in. By all of three votes. The right is split: more people voted for Cherniak than there were votes in the democratic bloc. And apparently not everyone from the democratic bloc voted, for Kotsiuba, surprisingly, was campaigning for Masol yesterday.

(Kotsiuba shocked the adherents of the democratic bloc with his speech. This was the second disillusionment associated with him. The first had to do with the story of the two boys, Berdnyk and Dukhovnikov, who were arrested on April 22 near the Lenin monument in Kiev. In the presence of Kotsiuba and the procurator, they wrote out a confession and were released from jail. Kotsiuba made a statement to this effect on the second day after his election as chairman of the judicial commission. There were many from the democratic bloc—Khmara, for instance—who vented their indignation about it in the corridors.)

The election of Masol seems a neat trick. In contrast to Cherniak, the partocrats decided not to saw off the branch they're sitting on, and chose Masol. However, I think they've cut off the branch with their own decision; Masol's government won't last long. A year or two, no longer. Then, perhaps, Cherniak's day will come. There's only one question: how to survive these two years? And what if it's five?

I was in a village in the Ternopil region for two days. It's surprising how closely people are following the sessions. In the regional center (the small town of Pidvolochysk), the blue-and-yellow flag hangs from the flagstaff. All around, from all sides, all the Lenins look down on this "indecency"—from the monument near the regional party committee (the largest building in town), from bas-reliefs, ghastly stands, honorary plaques. I counted five of them. For some reason, I began really to take notice of these Lenins and Leninoids. There are fewer slogans, but Lenins are conspicuous everywhere. Monstrous, bearing no resemblance to one another, produced by second-rate artists in the provinces, painted in a brilliant gold color, made of white plaster of Paris or styrofoam, hollow inside, like all our ideology.

The people here and in the surrounding villages whisper among themselves about whether there will be a free Ukraine. They believe in aid from the West. How naive! The Lithuanian story hasn't convinced them. In the town cafe, the local alcoholics quaff their vodka with the toast, "Glory to Ukraine!" The shops are bare, as everywhere. But one woman, who spent her childhood in internal exile with her parents, told me: "When I gaze upon our flag, I don't even think of eating." You can live a while on such idealism, but not for long, it seems to me.

June 28 (continued)

The television broadcast showed a number of interesting moments. Yuknovsky's declaration about the elections rang with the words, "conspiracy of the partocrats." The partocrats rushed from their places. Hurenko announced a protest in the name of the communists, while Kravchuk sat quietly. It was with much difficulty that Ivashko calmed them down.

Then the elections took place, which Masol won. Triumphantly, he accepted salutations, while Fokin, for some reason, suddenly withered away. Then they elected Yavorivsky and Ostapenko as chairs of the standing commissions. There were no particular complaints put to Yavorivsky. The right was none too eager to take up Chernobyl, knowing the danger there, and yielded this position without a fuss.

Then they began discussing the declaration of sovereignty. Drohuntsov, once an assistant to Liashko, the former prime minister—thus a "stagnation cadre," as we call such people around here—made an official proposal. In this proposal, at every turn one encountered the words USSR, Union treaty, and appeals to convoke a conference forthwith and draw up the treaty. (Somebody counted 11 references to the Union.) Then those who were, for the most part, critics of the proposal spoke up. Among them were Holovaty, Khmara, Kosiv and other democrats (I don't remember them all)—all of one mind that the question of drawing up a new treaty should be excluded from the declaration. Khmara was amazingly composed and calm, and said, among other things, that the name of our state should be changed back to the Ukrainian People's Republic. Hurenko spoke on behalf of the communist "For Soviet Ukraine" bloc. It has 239 members (out of a total of 450). This is significantly fewer than had been thought, but it gives them a majority. What they want is clear.

I cannot for the life of me figure out why they so much want this new treaty. It may yet emerge that it is the Ukrainians most loyal to Gorbachev's Moscow—not so long ago "Brezhnev's reserve," as Ukraine was popularly called—who are in such a rush to draw it up. It's worth noting that not even a year has passed since Gorbachev himself recommended Ivashko in Volodymyr Shcherbytsky's place. And that old dinosaur, Shcherbytsky, said at the time that no better successor was in view; that is, literally just before dying, physically and politically, he bequeathed Ivashko to the party, and to us. True, I think that he would be disappointed in Ivashko's subsequent actions.

Nevertheless, 239 people in Hurenko's bloc! The question need not be discussed, since it has already been decided in advance. The democratic bloc is clearly depressed by it.

The cameras showed the hall in which there are many dozing away. The legal subtleties that Holovaty employed, for instance, are considered suspicious, obscure and boring by the partocrats, all the more since they are already programmed to vote for particular motions. Among the partocrats sits the former secretary of the Central Committee, our "eminent" ideologue, Yelchenko, a pensioner for some days now, sunken-chested, aged, collapsed like a deflated rubber toy. Kravchuk, his former subordinate, by contrast has pushed himself up through the hierarchy, becoming the second secretary of the Central Committee. He appears suitably focused and seems to have become more youthful.

It's amazing how incredibly quickly the time goes. What yesterday was not even thought, let alone expressed, is today said out loud and becomes a subject of dispute. A year ago any discussion of a new Union treaty was the height of revolution. Today we have the open proclamation by representatives of the Narodna Rada that they are against the new treaty. And although there is no chance of success now, it seems that everything's been said. It's interesting to think about what will happen next.

July 1

Friday, the 29th, the second day of discussion on the Declaration of Sovereignty, likewise didn't pass without a scandal. Colonel Martyrosian,[33] a Russian-speaking Armenian, Rukh activist and Union deputy from the Rivne area, spoke very powerfully and agitatedly about the danger of an overthrow from the right, about the fact that in the army there are forces capable of shooting or imprisoning this whole parliament and any resembling it. (God, the life we live! Truly under the sword of Damocles, and yet we laugh, eat, drink, sleep, and write something). He called on the deputies to make very careful decisions, as it may already be late in the day.

After a couple more speakers, General Tolupko spoke. Besides being a reactionary, he declared that Col. Martyrosian should go back to Armenia and enlighten his own people. A hubbub broke out. Deputies rushed to the podium, surrounded it, and Pliushch, who was chairing, asked the general to quit the podium. Just like that. There was little satisfaction to be had from this, for Martyrosian's words were true. After this, Pliushch announced a break until Thursday, ostensibly for discussion of the declaration in commissions, but really to allow communist deputies to attend the 28th Congress of the CPSU in Moscow. Almost 60 deputies took off, not only the partocrats (there were also democrats such as Vitalii Karpenko, editor of *Vechirnii Kyiv*) from Ukraine, although, naturally, they were for the most part the higher echelons of party rulers.

Outside the Supreme Rada building the crowd is already much smaller than during the first days (I was there on Friday): four or five flags; some man with a megaphone. The deputies come out and, paying no attention to the modest gathering, scurry on, while the militia watches to make sure no one lays a hand on them. Onlookers crowd around the police barrier. The temperature is more than 30 degrees. It's stifling, oppressive, sultry, and no one can see the end of it.

Tomorrow the 28th Congress begins, but little is expected from it. There's not even any prognosis of an impending split. There are only 100 delegates from the Democratic Platform going. There are rumors that Yegor Ligachev and Aleksandr Yakovlev will retire, while Gorbachev stays on as General Secretary.

July 3

The 28th Congress of the CPSU began yesterday in Moscow. Probably they are showing it on your television. I've rather cooled off toward the affairs of my former party, but out of old habit read Gorbachev's report. Practically since childhood I've been accustomed to reading the reports of the general secretaries. At school and at university we were obliged to read them and almost to memorize them. Even today I can still remember bits of them.

This report was amazingly short, without long expositions about how much the economy will expand over the next five years. Nowadays such an assertion is only laughed at. But, quite proprietorially, Gorbachev spoke about the USSR's economic strategy, about the strategy in the villages, as though the CPSU were going to determine it. That is, the party considers itself a "ruling" party despite all the changes in the constitution. And in this report a new formula emerged: the party now is not in command but is avant-garde. Naturally, I was looking for something about the national question. And I found it—the party is to preserve its internationalist principles, for "in the provinces" separatists and nationalists are raising their heads. There are even those who are for a bourgeois regime. Give me a break!

The general secretary does not admit any possibility of the collapse of the Union; he speaks of a renewed federation as though of something perfectly obvious, if not already realized. (It only remains to subdue the separatists.) Is this blindness? Or a desire to bring history to a halt? It's hard to understand, but such a viewpoint is frightening. And what if they succeed? Like most of the people in my milieu, I too feel that this is, right now, the last chance for Ukraine.

In Moscow the commission writing the new treaty apparently is already at work. The treaty is for all of us. Moreover, it's amazing how firmly Gorbachev stands for "freedom of choice" for the former socialist countries of Eastern Europe. He guarantees them free choice and liberty, but offers the republics of the USSR only a treaty.

July 4

I spoke today with the deputy Bohdan Horyn,[34] a former political prisoner who is quite pessimistic about the chances of influencing the decision about the Ukrainian Declaration of Sovereignty. The most the democratic bloc can do is to torpedo the taking of a decision for a while. After all, most of the deputies are at the 28th Congress in Moscow and, without the democratic bloc, there is no quorum. I sensed a certain impotence in his mood, which is all too typical these days: the feeling of powerlessness to change anything today, right now. At the same time there's the feeling that tomorrow will be too late.

Yesterday, *Vechirnii Kyiv* (Evening Kiev) published the declaration of the delegates of the "Democratic Platform in the CPU." It testifies to their disappointment with the results of the first half of the CPU congress. And the other congress, now going on in Moscow, has likewise proved disappointing right from the start. Basically, I expected nothing from it, but the idea of a "communist perspective," as evoked in Gorbachev's speech, will probably satisfy only the right.

Several newspapers, for instance *Izvestiia* and *Vechirnii Kyiv*, express a certain skepticism about the congress. Something rather suspicious is going on with the press. Some papers just don't arrive, as a rule the ones which are most critical with respect to the regime, such as *Komsomolskaia Pravda*. It hasn't been around for weeks. Everything's in order, though, with *Pravda* and *Radianska Ukraina*. It's odd how for some papers there's enough newsprint, for others not.

What's particularly interesting to me is whether the "Democratic Platform" is going to leave the CPSU and what Yeltsin is going to say in his speech.

In Kiev these days the most striking thing is the constant queuing at the jewellery stores. Dozens, hundreds of people want to buy gold and diamonds, and will stand around for days in the heat in the hope of doing so. At the jeweller's that I pass every day there is a notice that in a few days there will be an auction of diamonds valued at more than 8,000 rubles. At the same time the grocery stores are utterly empty.

A general political strike of the miners is drawing closer. The press isn't exactly publicizing their demands, but evidently among them is a call for the resignation of the government. Such are our affairs.

A word about the threat of a right-wing coup.

Just now—it's 1:00 a.m.—on Central Television, they interviewed General Gromov, commander of the Kiev military district and a delegate to the party congress. He praised Ligachev's speech. Ligachev is "concerned" about the army and said that the army without the party is an impossibility and, most importantly, that the army is the bearer of morality. In Russia there's always been a great feeling for the army. It's obvious that for him Ukraine is at best *okraina* (the frontier) of Russia. And the Communist party? The unjust object of attack by those who aspire to the seizure of power.

Today's speeches in response to Gorbachev's report had an ominous character. Not that the report pleased me—not a single thoughtful proposal about how to get out of the crisis— but when people criticize it for its departures from Marxism-

Leninism, this is really frightening.

You may be wondering why I, an aesthete, am so taken up with party congresses. The reason is simple: I'm calculating the chances of a coup d'état.

July 6

As usual, I am writing these Dostoevskian "notes from the house of the dead" late at night. We're having an incredible heat wave; it's more than 30 degrees on the street and you can imagine, with our humidity, it's sheer hell. Nevertheless, on October Revolution Square[35]—what a name!—the trade in samizdat goes on as usual, and I, returning from work, bought something, as always. It seems that the liveliest trade is in the various pamphlets and newsletters of the Ukrainian Republican party (URP). Today I took note of an aging hippie in T-shirt and shorts. For our conservative society, to walk in the streets in shorts is a kind of dissidence all its own; once the militia stopped me when I went into a shop in shorts. As for the hippie: behind him, under a tree, there was a blue-and-yellow flag with a greenish tint to the blue, perhaps as a sign of support for the Greens; and a trident of colossal proportions. He was selling the URP paper and a dozen different pins, from a Banderist pin to a Pioneer pin with Lenin on it; and for all that he was speaking Russian. What marvelous eclecticism! Standing not far off, a banner with the words: Crimean Tatars for a Free Ukraine. The situation in the Crimea is rather complicated. Conservative forces are being mobilized there which, hiding behind the Tatars, who not so long ago weren't even allowed to go there, aspire to Crimean autonomy.

Here in the square the newspapers of the Ukrainian social democrats have made their appearance, in the Russian language. These social democrats have a clear pro-Russian bent, even though they too are apparently anti-Union. I haven't quite figured them out. It's even hard to say how many there are of them. They had their founding congress in Kiev in May in that very same, much-heralded Polytechnical Institute. All in all, there are congresses going on everywhere in Ukraine right now. And they're all "founding."

On June 9 in Kiev the Ukrainian Peasant Democratic party had its founding congress. They adopted a program and statutes, elected four directors, among them the writer Serhii Plachynda, and adopted a Declaration of Basic Principles that *Literaturna Ukraina* recently published. The declaration was very literary, especially in its first section, which is titled "History"; in general, all the serious parties and movements have up to now been organized and run by writers, and among the official newspapers only *Literaturna Ukraina* has been publishing all the oppositional materials. The Peasant party is a party of farmers, even though farmers don't exist yet as a social group, and it has a pronounced religious slant, although they emphasize that atheists can be members. At its heart is the cult of the mother: "to nurture the YOUNG UKRAINIAN MOTHER" (quoted from *Literaturna Ukraina* for July 5), and a call to "revive the ancient cult of Berehynia, the original goddess of domestic harmony." About equality and feminism, there is naturally not a word. This is perhaps historically explicable by our poverty, ignorance and the destruction that "socialism" has wrought among our people. Therefore, to move forward it appears that again we have to make a step backward. The religious spirit and pathos—there is on the whole a lot of pathos in the declaration—are most evident in the last section, "Prayer." "We will have neither our own path nor a destiny nor a soul without Thee, OUR MERCI-FUL AND ALL-POWERFUL LORD... It is we, Lord, Ukrainian peasants, your children, who have gathered together under the blue-and-yellow banner,..." etc. There is no sort of elaborated economic program. Nevertheless, there is movement, movement everywhere. And that, maybe, is the most important thing.

The All-Ukrainian Association of Doctors had their founding congress on June 30. One more Ukrainian organization.

At this very time (July 3, 4, 5), the Synod (enough already with these pompous names!) of the Ukrainian Spiritual Republic is being conducted in Kolomyia in the Ivano-Frankivsk area. What it is is not exactly clear. Initiating and inspiring all this has been Oles Berdnyk, the former dissident and notorious God-seeker. While the democratic bloc is struggling for an independent Ukraine, he has established his spiritual republic. It's to be found somewhere in the heavens. At Rukh's Great Council, they laughed at this "impulse toward the cosmic," and today at the session of the Supreme Rada Levko Lukia-nenko, who had been there, talked about it rather skeptically. As he put it, in order to direct the Synod from the cosmic to the mundane and ideologically correct path.

The pathos of the main document of the Synod, a "Char-ter of Freedom of the Ukrainian Spiritual Republic," is un-equalled, even on the Ukrainian scale. For example: "Children of Sacred Ukraine! Children of the Spiritual Nations! Let's prepare our wings!" Or the beginning: "The world spiritual revolution is nigh," or "Holy Ukraine affirms that not only those now carrying on an earthly existence, but also the dead and the unborn Children of Mother Ukraine, are subjects according to law, as the Great Kobzar [Shevchenko][36] reminds us." And so on, in the same style, pretensions to a new utopia or a new religion.

On the whole, God-seeking, mysticism, astrology, palmist-ry and various sorts of magic are incredibly popular among us. This is the newest sign of the times, the biggest fad. Everybody believes in ESP and different kinds of shamanism. For more than two weeks some sort of travelling fortune-teller gave healing seances at the Kiev stadium for 100,000 at one time. It was impossible to get tickets—speculators charged 50 rubles above face value for them on the black market. Not 100,000 but 150,000 people from all over Ukraine were packed into the stadium in that dreadful heat. Tales have been told of how, right at the stadium, paralyzed people got up and walked. Some individual skeptics, it's true, laughed at this, but where are people supposed to get treated when there isn't even aspirin in the shops?

Another sign of the times—excuse me for skipping like this from the sublime to the ridiculous—is pornography.

Calendars and crude postcards with half-naked and naked girls are sold everywhere; in some paper just yesterday I saw a reprint of photos of Soviet girls from *Playboy*. When I, as a feminist, got angry about this, one of my women friends—an exemplary mother, a communist and a faithful spouse—said, "What's your problem? I'm really happy for these poor girls, that they've got the chance to make some money. At least they'll see a bit of happiness in life."

On Shevchenko Boulevard a small private gallery, the Art Salon, opened recently. An enormous sign—"Exhibit of Erotic Photography"—is now hanging on the door. Rather cheap and pretentious framed photographs in one small room. What was interesting was that there were virtually only men in the room. These exhibits have become quite a popular and profitable business. I should say that almost no one supports me in my criticism of the flood of pornography which is being sold all over the place—for example, in the central underground crossing in downtown Kiev, underneath October Revolution Square itself (what a name! still!). It signifies that I'm some kind of philistine and conservative. Perhaps only the reactionary communist Egor Kuzmich Ligachev would support me, but without any sincerity.

Everything's more or less peaceful today at the Supreme Rada, although it's true that they are raising the question of "openness" rather sharply: the deputies are in a rage that *Radianska Ukraina* finds space to publish the speeches from the Moscow Party Congress, but for an elucidation of the sessions there's just not enough newsprint.

Mind you, peace and quiet are relative. The threat of a general political strike of the miners of the USSR hangs over the partocrats like a black cloud. The party and government call on them not to strike, but they are insistent: they're preparing for it. So they resolved at their first congress, which was held not long ago. In a special resolution about the CPSU they wrote that they don't consider the party to be theirs. They demand the nationalization of its property, the resignation of the Union government and the depoliticization of the state organs. Yemets, chairman of the human rights commission of the Supreme Rada, proposed the setting up of a group that would appraise party property and indicate ways of nationalizing it. And so that's where it's heading. Nevertheless we're in for troubled times. Is it possible that they could get even more unsettling?

There's growing dissatisfaction at the absence of many deputies from the meetings. Why precisely did Ivashko abandon the Supreme Rada for the ten days of the CPSU Congress? Maybe he wanted to signal to us that for him it was more important than his job? The answer is obvious. Yeltsin spoke at the CPSU congress and then disappeared to sit in the Russian parliament. It is not clear what he said. But it seems that it didn't create too much of a sensation. One of the miner-deputies wrote a note to the Supreme Rada chairman, Pliushch, that he was leaving for the Donbas to go on strike. And maliciously added that the party oblast committee secretary from his delegation was in Moscow for the congress of the CPSU.

July 7

Today is Saturday and there's hardly any news. It's the sixth day of the CPSU Congress, but that's not news. Today Central Television reported on the potential conflict between Ukraine and Moldova over Bessarabia. Moldova is demanding that part of Odessa oblast be returned to it and that it be united, along with Moldova, with Romania. Agents from Moldova are travelling there and agitating for it. Central Television broadcast a provocative rumor that Moldova was conducting some kind of negotiations with Rukh. I don't think that anybody in Rukh intends to give up any territory or has the mandate to do it. A diplomat of my acquaintance, of rather high rank, said recently that we might be opening an embassy somewhere, but that with Moldova there might not be any diplomatic relations at all. As though he could see ahead.

On the whole the central press seems to be printing the truth, but not without certain tendencies. *Komsomolskaia Pravda,* one of the Moscow papers "on the left," printed a short notice from Lviv about the declaration of the leader of the Union of National Ukrainian Youth (UNUY), which was totally fascistic in character. (The Ukrainian nation is the best in the world; it is meant to rule over others, etc.) I don't know how much is true in this, how much is false, but Mister Youth Leader, as reported in the Moscow press, pronounced some pretty scary slogans. On the whole the UNUY and the Ukrainian National party (UNP) (I think they have the same people in their leadership) are a dangerous deviation. However, they're not at all numerous (I read in *Kommersant* that there are 12 members in the UNP). But they make a big deal of it in Moscow. It's obvious why: to show the face of the enemy. The civil war that has been going on for 72 years isn't over yet. "Perestroika" is bait for foreigners. Among us the main point is finding the enemy—and along with him, those close to him: they live in the same city, they too criticize the CPSU, or something else in that vein.

What Vynnychenko[37] wrote in *Rebirth of a Nation* is now being repeated. The Russian democrat is no democrat at all on the Ukrainian question. This was in 1917, after the February revolution, and then the October revolution. We have the same thing now.

July 18

I returned yesterday from ten days in a village in the Carpathians. Today I'll be in Moscow; day after tomorrow, London. My head's whirling with all the things I still have to do.

It's almost impossible to be a chronicler of the political movement in Ukraine. From morning to night you have to sit down and write, and I just don't have the strength for it. On top of that there's my work, articles, translations, my obligations to publishers. I don't know how much longer I can keep up this writing.

So, what's been happening since July 7?

Extraordinary changes. On the 11th, the all-Union political strike of the miners took place and the CPSU congress concluded. Ivashko fled from Kiev in disgrace when Gorbachev lured him to Moscow to become deputy General Secretary and finally, on July 16, the Supreme Rada of Ukraine adopted the declaration on Ukraine's sovereignty. Now we have an Independence Day, but I doubt, somehow, that the "big" world out there has noticed.

Early on July 11, Ivan Stepanovych (not Mazepa[38] but Pliushch), Ivashko's first deputy, read out Ivashko's statement of resignation as head of parliament. It was dated the 9th and read out on the 11th, because there was no plenary session on the 10th. His explanation was unconvincing and awkward. The Supreme Rada recalled all the delegate-deputies from the CPSU congress, Ivashko among them. He "took offence" at this lack of trust and resigned. In reality, it was on the very same 11th that Gorbachev recommended Ivashko for the position of his deputy in the party, and on the 12th he was already elected. Essentially, the deputy will now direct the work of the CPSU and the general secretary will be occupied with presidential affairs. Ivashko, in spite of some derision in the hall (there, at the congress), won out over his "weaker" competitors, among them Ligachev, who has finally bowed off the political stage.

The Supreme Rada deputies sat in a state of evident shock at the announcement. Even now they haven't altogether shaken it off. The partocrats were taken completely by surprise. How hard they had fought for Ivashko to lead the Supreme Rada, and how easily he betrayed them! But in the end all this proved useful and, although the Rada is now "headless," in Ivan Drach's word, this in itself facilitated in the adoption of the sovereignty declaration in a version that would never have passed two months ago.

The Supreme Rada debated every sentence—literally every comma—over the course of a week, and on Friday, the 13th, completed it. And on Monday morning it adopted the entire text.

But let me go back. Blue-and-yellow flags were in evidence at the miners' strike in Donetsk. They were very visible on the television news, and that's the most pleasant development. However, the party ignores the miners' demands. Their principal demand is for the nationalization of party property and the dissolution of party and Komsomol committees in the mines. In the future, this official indifference is going to lead to terrible cataclysms.

Members are still leaving the party, among them such important figures as Yeltsin. He made his announcement at the congress on the 12th and quit the hall to the accompaniment of applause and whistles. The mayors of Moscow and Leningrad have left the party.

But how will things develop from here? There's an enormous gap between the Declaration of Sovereignty and the declared Program of the CPSU congress. The CPSU, as though this were its business, is insisting that the new Union treaty be signed by the end of the year. This is frightening, although there are many who don't believe it's possible now to draft a treaty that would satisfy all parties. The declaration proclaimed the necessity for national armed forces, but the program insists on the "exclusive competence of the Union" with regard to armed forces, and so on. There's an ocean of such inconsistencies. It's impossible to know what will happen tomorrow.

I still have piles of information from western Ukraine, where, as of the first of July, the first independent newspapers are coming out—*Za Vilnu Ukrainu* (For a Free Ukraine) in Lviv and *Halychyna* (Galicia) in Ivano-Frankivsk; where, in Drohobych, they've already put up a monument to Stepan Bandera; where on every village council office there hangs the blue-and-yellow flag. But I'll tell you all about this in my next letter.

July 29

I don't know how you found your trip home from England, but my return was quite dramatic. I was sad on leaving Harrogate and London. At Heathrow I started to feel really depressed. My depression began when our group, which attended the World Congress of Soviet and East European Studies, was overtaken by a number of parliamentary deputies from Russia, badges of office on their lapels, pushing a mountain of video cassette recorders on a cart—obviously more than one for each of their relatives. It was quite a comic spectacle: Russian parliamentarians in formal suits and ties pushing for all they were worth, bending double to roll Western equipment into the land of "democratic socialism."

Then the airplane was delayed for several hours because a passenger had checked his luggage but failed to board. Some of the English passengers were frightened of terrorists and wanted to deplane. But after a baggage check of the entire plane that took several hours, we somehow managed to take off.

In the plane I found an issue of *Sovetskaia Rossiia* (Soviet Russia), and the first article I began to read reported the laying of charges against General Kalugin, a former KGB operative who is now criticizing his home institution. The article stated that separatism was becoming official policy "in the borderlands"; that it was becoming necessary to protect the Russian population, again "in the borderlands." My mood grew blacker. Immediately I had a reprise of the persistent feeling that all this could end. "All this" meaning perestroika—I hate the word, but can't think of a better one. This unpleasant feeling disappeared for a while in England, perhaps under the influence of the general optimism in the British press and of the sovietologists I heard at the congress, who were mostly enthused about perestroika and Gorbachev.

At Sheremetevo airport our passports were checked by murky customs officers and we walked out onto a gloomy street to see a long lineup for taxis. Not a car in sight. With great difficulty, we managed to hire a decrepit bus for 50 rubles and followed a murky, poorly lit road into the city. Suddenly the bus made a zigzag to avoid a woman's corpse. In the dim lamplight I managed to glimpse a white blouse, bare feet and a pool of blood. There were two cars nearby. The driver who had killed the woman had taken off. The bus driver, along with my colleagues Syvokin and Zhulynsky, got off the bus while I sat rooted to my seat. My bad mood had turned catastrophically awful. We reached the filthy railway station, which was crowded—nowhere to stand, let alone sit down. We happened to buy tickets for a train that was leaving in fifteen minutes. Living here, you learn to take satisfaction in the slightest piece of good luck. And so, feeling happy in spite of the incredible filth in the train, we rattled on home.

At home a new surprise awaited me. Kiev was in a panic. A blob of phenol which had spilled into the Desna, a tributary of the Dnieper, somewhere near Briansk, was expected to reach the city. There was a message from my parents on the table warning me not to drink the water. The huge blob of phenol was making its way to Kiev slowly but relentlessly. Furious, I thought, "How long is all this going to go on?"

But at least I was home in Kiev, and, regardless of the phenol, I began to feel like myself again. At the station we had been met by Tolia Shpytal, who works in our institute. He was waving the latest issue of *Kultura i zhyttia* (Culture and Life), which carried a report on the raising of the blue-and-yellow colors at the city council building on Khreshchatyk on July 24. He had been there and told us that a crowd of 120,000 gathered at the meeting.

I very much wanted to see the flag. Even if a symbol's value is merely symbolic, it still means a great deal. I reached the spot at 9:00 p.m. The flagpole was a tall one, and the flag was huge. It's hard to believe! In the ten days that I was away from Kiev, our democratic forces had taken yet another stride forward. Near the base of the flagpole there was a crowd of people with flags, and an endless meeting seems to be going on. The flagpole is surrounded with flowers, blue-and-yellow flags, postcards and banners with slogans. (There were also a couple of wilted flowers by the Soviet flag, probably brought by old Bolsheviks.)

I returned along the same street from my parents' house at 11:00 p.m. There were fewer people, but still a fairly large number. I hear that there are people in the area 24 hours a day. They stand there and sing folk songs while the old Soviet flag hangs rather somberly on the neighboring flagpole. I heard that the communists are going from one building authority to another and gathering signatures on petitions to take down the national flag. In fact, city council was without a quorum when it adopted the resolution to raise the national flag. The parto-crats tried to make an issue of this at first, but now it would probably be impossible to take down the flag.

This afternoon in Kiev there was a big meeting near the Lenin monument on October Revolution Square. The organiz-ers were the radical Interparty assembly, whose goal is to close down the Chernobyl nuclear station. On the 9th there is to be a general city-wide strike to support this demand. There was a report about this meeting on the television news program, which showed former sailors singing and playing guitars, because it's Navy Day. The correspondent asked them some-thing about their attitude to politics and the Declaration on Ukrainian Sovereignty, and they told him drunkenly that they support a free Ukraine and a Ukrainian fleet on the Black Sea.

But to speak seriously, the situation is rather piquant. Since July 23, the head of parliament has been Leonid Krav-chuk, member of the CPU Politburo and a recent opponent of Rukh.

Finally the Supreme Rada accepted the resignation of Ivashko, who exchanged his post as head of the Rada for that of Gorbachev's deputy in the CPSU. What phenomenal lack of foresight! He came in for a great deal of criticism, and Oles Shevchenko even proposed that he be deprived of Ukrainian citizenship.

Nominations for a new chairman proceeded in nervous fashion. There were 27 candidates, from Holovaty and Khmara to Pliushch and Hurenko—the greatest democrats and the greatest conservatives. Then the members took fright. How long would the elections drag on if they were obliged to listen to 27 programs? And pressure was put on candidates to withdraw their names.

But most candidates nevertheless presented their pro-grams.

Yukhnovsky, the leader of the opposition, already making his second programmatic speech, had a clear message and made the best presentation. He was the only one to whom people listened attentively. It is interesting that he has shifted his position on the Union treaty. Two months ago he spoke about "Ukraine within the borders of the Union," for which he was criticized by even more "left-wing" members of the Narodna Rada. Now he was saying that the treaty could be signed only after Ukraine had constituted itself as a sovereign state.

In discussion, Yukhnovsky's speech attracted most of the favorable remarks. But he had no chance whatever of being elected, since the "bloc of 239" was quietly going about its business.

Kravchuk's speech was extremely poor. He had no program whatever. He swore his loyalty to the party and said that he would not allow anticommunism in the auditorium. He said that he would not follow Yeltsin's example and leave the party. Hurenko said more or less the same. But it was clear that Kravchuk could say whatever he pleased. He had the support of the party majority, which would elect him in any case.

Holovaty was one of the first to withdraw his candidacy, but he did so with éclat, as always, speaking somewhat rhetorically and presenting an original analysis of parliament's inability to guarantee Ukraine's state sovereignty, since it had already elected the communist Ivashko.

Many others withdrew their candidacies, leaving five men in the running.

The debate took on the form of a political discussion about communism and anticommunism, not normal parliamentary procedure. The members of the democratic bloc used their time to agitate against the Union treaty, while the communists responded by agitating for it. This is the main issue and has now become the principal criterion for determining a member's position.

No one was elected on the first round of balloting. Kravchuk obtained 224 votes and Yukhnovsky 140, while the others (Artemenko, Pravdenko, Mokin) took a negligible quantity. This was a great disappointment, although it had been expected. True, it remains a mystery why Kravchuk obtained only 224 votes, since the bloc "For Soviet Ukraine" consists of 239 members. Yukhnovsky then withdrew his candidacy. Accordingly, two candidates were left, Kravchuk and Mokin (the latter receiving 19 votes in the first round).

Only 315 votes were cast in the second round (407 had been cast in the first). Kravchuk won the fatal 239 and was elected.

After the election, to the accompaniment of noise and foot-stamping, D[mytro] P[avlychko] declared that the Narodna Rada had boycotted the second round of voting and took no responsibility for the election of Kravchuk. The communists drove D[mytro] P[avlychko] from the podium. That is to say, he did not finish his statement, but left the platform under the assault of terrible noise.

D[mytro] P[avlychko] later told me that not all the members of the Narodna Rada had taken part in the boycott, and this, in his view, had created a quorum for Kravchuk's election.

By the way, the candidates' declarations on the women's question were astounding—return women to their place in the home; women should only be mothers; and one (Khmelniuk, first secretary of the Odessa city party committee) said that a law should be passed forbidding women to work more than four hours. I thought to myself, "How long do I work?" Ten? Fifteen hours? But a "serious" man, a member of parliament, tells me that I should not write and translate but sit at home. This when some of my male colleagues at the institute are alcoholics or do-nothings. Our communist party is unredeemable. First it passes a law telling all women to work; now it wants to prohibit them from doing so.

The ministers are now being elected. True, Prime Minister Masol doesn't even want to hear of a Ministry of Defense,[39] even though D[mytro] P[avlychko] gave an interview to *Izvestiia* in which he said that we would have our own army. A large group (28, including Hryniov, whose popularity has grown lately) has left the CPSU.

Hryniov has returned from Moscow, where he was

attending a meeting of the Soviet of the Federation to debate the prospects of a Union treaty. Gorbachev and Ryzhkov are demanding that it be drafted in a month and a half and signed in December 1990 at a session of the USSR Supreme Soviet. The "center" is proposing rather humiliating conditions. The pressure and haste on Moscow's part are incredible, and the prospects unclear.

July 30

Today the Supreme Rada is continuing to "roast" the ministers. By no means do all of them inspire confidence.

The morning session was very intense. There was a debate on the recall of 10,000 soldiers of the internal forces who are serving outside Ukraine in areas of inter-ethnic strife. The mothers' protests are mounting, since Ukrainian boys are dying in Kirghizia and Transcaucasia. Despite protests from the generals, it was decided to recall them as of September 1.

There was also an incident at the end of the session during the debate on "other business." The first secretary of the Chernihiv oblast committee protested the decision of the oblast committee to end the teaching of Russian in the first years of secondary schools. There was a storm of protest. Iryna Kalynets (a well-known former political prisoner), who was dressed in an elegant blue gown, conducted with both hands when the democratic bloc stood as a body to shout, "Shame!" Then they all threw themselves at the podium literally to drive Lisovenko away. Hryniov, who was chairing the session, barely succeeded in calming the auditorium.

Then Porovsky spoke about the 500th anniversary of Cossackdom, which is to be celebrated from 2 to 7 August, and said that Rukh, the URP and the democratic bloc are the heirs of the Cossacks. It ended, of course, with the national anthem, "Long live Ukraine."

The member from Dniprodzerdzhynsk proposed that the mandates of delegates to all-Union bodies from Ukraine be revoked. Lithuania did the same with its deputies long ago.

Moreover, in the town of Ordzhonikidze, Dnipropetrovsk oblast, the city council raised a blue-and-yellow flag two days ago. This is noteworthy. Ordzhonikidze, in the industrial, Russified region of Ukraine, is not Lviv, or even Kiev.

As always, there is as much of interest behind the scenes as on the political stage.

The Narodna Rada was in session tonight. New elections were held. Yukhnovsky was again elected leader of the opposition, although there were other nominations (the most radical members wanted a change of leader). There are five deputy heads: Lukianenko, Pavlychko, Filenko, Larysa Skoryk, and Mykhailo Horyn. All of them, as well as six members-at-large, constitute the Presidium of the Narodna Rada.

There was also a meeting of the "Soviet Ukraine" bloc. The situation is becoming more and more tense, and is reaching a crisis in connection with Moscow's pressure to sign a Union treaty. Earlier the democratic bloc intended to delay debate on this question as long as possible, i.e., not to follow the Lithuanian path, but its own, slower and calmer one. D[mytro] P[avlychko] said today that the democratic bloc would insist on the adoption of a constitution as a first step, for how can a state which has no constitution sign treaties? Then there should be some time to get used to the new constitution and see whether a treaty is actually required. If this fails, the Narodna Rada favors quitting parliament in the event that a treaty is signed and ratified.

Today D[mytro] P[avlychko] made a good joke: "We can accept President Gorbachev only in the role that the Queen of England plays in, say, Australia." But that is today. Tomorrow, I think, even that role will seem too great to him.

But there is also a concept of the treaty that is being proposed "from below"—a treaty to create a commonwealth that would require no "center," neither Gorbachev nor Ryzhkov.

Tomorrow there is a meeting to discuss Chernobyl. I am flying to the Carpathians tomorrow, so my next letter will be written upon my return in 7 to 10 days.

August 11

Today I returned from the Carpathians, where it's very hot. Under the blazing sun there bloomed blue-and-yellow flags, even on gas stations. But even without the heat, the Ivano-Frankivsk region is boiling. To begin with, there is an actual religious war going on between the Uniate Catholics[40] and Orthodox autocephalists. Village is pitted against village; relative against relative. It is quite common for priests to be stoned. In neighboring Chernivtsi oblast Russians and autocephalist Orthodox are feuding. None of this engenders optimism. Evidently our compatriots have a genetic tendency to fight one another. Of course, this campaign is being purposely stirred up and inflamed.

Secondly, Galicia is reading and passing from hand to hand the new official independent newspapers—*Halychyna* and *Za vilnu Ukrainu*. The Republican party is quite popular. Anticommunist feelings are hardening as the well-shafts filled with victims of the NKVD are excavated. There are several of these in the Ivano-Frankivsk region. In the village of Yabluniv in the Kosiv region the Memorial Society has unearthed about 100 corpses around the building where the NKVD was located. In 1945 my father also spent a few months in this building. He managed to survive because he was sent with a group of local youths to Ivano-Frankivsk for interrogation and trial. Scores of people were killed here. I have just come from the area, which is in a state of continual distress. Every day new skeletons are exhumed; every Sunday there are services for the dead; candles burn; volunteers work free of charge.

Thirdly, on a more cheerful note, I am struck by the dynamism of the shadow economy in Galicia. Everyone is taking "tourist" trips to Romania, Hungary, Yugoslavia, Poland, etc. They sell, buy, resell, then exchange socialist currency for dollars, buy goods again for dollars, then sell their acquisitions in Russia, and so it goes without end. There is nothing left in the stores. Everything that could be sold somewhere in Romania or Poland has already been bought up. Everyone talks of dinars, złoty, forints and dollars, and keeps the exchange value of all the currencies in his head.

In the village I followed parliamentary debates on television. For the hungry people, these broadcasts are their greatest recreation. They were also my biggest thrill during my holiday. Parliament concluded its first session in Kiev on August 3. It has gone into recess until October. In the last few days several more ministers have been elected. Our friend Zhulynsky, alas, failed to obtain the post of minister of culture. He did himself in on a question about Lenin. In Chervonohrad the city council had just adopted a resolution to take down the statue of Lenin. When asked about his attitude on the question, he did not condemn the action, as the majority—for whom Lenin is still an icon—would have wanted. Neither did he approve the decision—he was defeated by his fence-sitting. The rector of the Poltava pedagogical institute, Ziaziun, a most unpleasant person, was elected minister of education. Until recently he was still conducting a policy of Russification in Poltava, preparing teachers for Uzbekistan, and so on—it's obvious in which language. Generally speaking, the ministers, along with Masol, are an utterly disappointing lot. I think the best of them is the Olympic champion Borzov, the minister of sport. But what can Borzov offer the people under current conditions? Jogging on an empty stomach?

Over the past few days the question of Chernobyl was debated and two laws adopted, one giving village development a higher priority and another on economic independence. I don't know how the village is supposed to develop with collective farms. It's summer, and once again the papers are full of the usual—wheat is withering, tomatoes are rotting, there is no one to harvest them, we must wage a struggle for the harvest, and so on. As always, the CPU is adopting fervent resolutions and calling on everyone to go out to the fields. An endless spectacle of the absurd. Cherniak (the unsuccessful opposition candidate for premier) is right to repeat that our economy is an economy of the absurd, and it effortlessly proves this every day.

The session ended with two scandals. The bloc of 239

proposed a resolution protesting the removal of the statue of Lenin in Chervonohrad. The democratic bloc prevented a vote on the issue. All this took place in stormy fashion, with members rising and leaving the auditorium.

By the way, I learned from some member's speech that in the Lviv region there are about 500 busts and statues of Lenin. And Ukraine has 25 oblasts. A figure has been cited—I heard it from Drach—that there are 55,000 Lenin monuments in Ukraine. Once our classic writer Mykola Bazhan wrote a whole book about *Monuments to Lenin in Ukraine*. The partocrats are hysterical about the destruction of Lenins. The same thing happened with the monument in Ternopil. There were thousands of people at this "transfer" of Lenin to the oblast party committee. The CPU Central Committee adopted a resolution of protest. Today *Pravda* has a front-page scare story about vandals and extremists, saying that the CPU will stand by its people, etc. I heard that Lviv oblast committee secretary Sekretariuk said that he will buy with his own money the Lenin monument that was taken down. It just isn't clear where he would put it up.

The last day of the first session of parliament, August 3, was very difficult. Kravchuk proposed the formation of two commissions to draft a Ukrainian constitution, as well as Union and inter-republican treaties. The composition of these commissions was the subject of debate. Kravchuk proposed 25 oblast executive committee heads out of a total of 50 members. Someone with "communist naiveté" immediately proposed the addition of the commanders of Ukraine's three military districts. Someone from the democratic bloc responded ironically that the full complement of the Carpathian military district should be placed on the committee's roster. It was Kravchuk's idea that the constitution be drafted by the heads of oblast executive committees, most of whom are secretaries of communist party organizations. There were proposals from the floor to include a number of democrats, all of whom, including Shcherbak, lost in the balloting. When Holovaty refused to take part in the commission, others, such as Karpenko and Chornovil, followed his example. Thus a group was formed to prepare an alternative draft. So the question was not actually resolved.

It was the same with the second commission. Kravchuk, puffing his cheeks, tried to frighten people by saying that there were some opposed to the Union treaty (in the Presidium of the Supreme Rada there were 6 heads of commissions opposed to the treaty) and proceeded to explain what a boon the treaty was. He repeated this in his address to the nation on August 7. Some of the members noted that Kravchuk thinks one way in the morning and another after lunch. He has lunch on the very next street at the Central Committee of the CPU.

There is a tremendous campaign in favor of the Union treaty in the Moscow press and television. I am concerned about this question, although there are sensible people who do not believe in the possibility of the treaty's ratification. I do not share their optimism, and I would consider ratification a catastrophe. I am not the only one. Gorbachev is applying tremendous pressure. Obviously, he has grasped that if it is impossible to save the party, one should at least save the empire.

A couple of days ago the newspapers reported a truce between Gorbachev and Yeltsin. It is not clear on what conditions this was struck and what it portends. Most probably it has to do with the treaty, which Gorbachev wants so much and which cannot be adopted without Russia. For the time being he remains head of the party, which is utterly unpopular, and president of a state that is illegal and disintegrating.

At the beginning of August the festival of Cossack glory took place in Zaporizhzhia and the Dnipropetrovsk region. Half the democratic bloc was there, and Pliushch was the official representative of parliament. He was not well received when he spoke of "Soviet Ukraine," but was applauded when he followed what is now accepted tradition and ended with "Glory to Ukraine!" Moscow Radio maliciously reported that the Rukh leaders had exploited the festival for their own political ends.

D[mytro] P[avlychko] told me the following. The festival was attended by 200,000 people (other sources say 700,000).

Hundreds of busloads of people came from Western Ukraine. These enormous columns stirred the imagination. The whole event was very well organized: the enormous mass of people left not one scrap of paper or bottle to be cleared away. During the principal meeting at Zaporizhzhia a Cossack sat above the crowd atop a tall mill and, as they said, warded off the clouds, because it looked like rain, but in the end there was no rain. The well-known opera singer Mokrenko arrived in Cossack gear and did not even take off his cap, although it was extremely hot. There were many people in Cossack dress—one of them kept losing his glued-on mustache—and, of course, there was a sea of flags. People in the villages greeted their guests with enthusiasm, but it was different in the cities. In Zaporizhzhia the column paraded through the city, Rukh leaders at the head of the column handing out blue-and-yellow badges. Some people accepted them gratefully. Others demonstratively threw them on the ground or slapped their children's hands when they tried to take the badges. But in general, it was a great success. Of course, you could see the whole thing as a patriotic masquerade that is far from an objective understanding of Cossackdom, its historical role, and so on, but as a masquerade it obliged the residents of Zaporizhzhia and Dnipropetrovsk to reflect on their identity.

The members of parliament have gone home. Since May 15 they have all aged and their faces are drawn. On television the lines on their faces and their fatigue are evident. Some are in hospitals recovering. D[mytro] P[avlychko] is pale and worn out with exhaustion. All of us are concerned about him.

In Kiev and Lviv there is an international physicians' congress. A few days ago they had a big meeting with members of parliament in the Kiev Cinema Building. The speech was given by the poet and member of parliament Petro Osadchuk, who has a wonderful sense of humor. He was asked about his attitude to Borys Oliinyk, the stalwart literary apparatchik who has attacked Rukh. Osadchuk began to praise him: Oliinyk's recent article was so good and convincing that it made me leave the Communist party! When the democrat Osadchuk, who is well known in the literary milieu for his deadly epigrams, began to praise Oliinyk, the auditorium fell silent. Oliinyk is extremely unpopular. A few days ago he gave a press conference in Kiev to say that he would be with the CPSU to the end and saved his severest criticism for the "opportunists" who had deserted the party in its "dark hour." The veiled reference to his fellow writers was evident. It was they who, in his opinion, were least to be trusted.

August 16

Kiev seems quiet. It could hardly be otherwise—it is 30 degrees outside. The heat is extraordinarily persistent and enervating. Parliament is in recess. The politicians have gone off in all directions. People are apathetic; even their hatred for the Gorbachev-Ryzhkov government, which appears to enjoy no esteem whatever, is somehow apathetic and lax.

From time to time in Kiev there are tobacco strikes. Men picket Red Army Street near the central Kiev tobacco store. Prices are rising, and gas lines are growing longer—they are already a kilometer long and it is utterly pointless to wait in them. Also, there is a greater number of pornographic posters, which are being sold in every underground crossing by suspicious types. It seems that these, as well as video stores selling pirated copies of films about American fighters, are the only flourishing and legal businesses.

Despite the heat, there is always a crowd by the blue-and-yellow flag near city council. I met my friend Maksym Strikha, a member of the Kiev city council, there. Whenever he has some time free from physics and council business, he manages to do translations for a book of selected poems of Emily Dickinson that I am preparing for publication. I am impressed by his council member's badge. Half the members of city council wear their badges with a flag, no longer the Soviet but the national one. Maksym, though a physicist, is utterly embroiled in the religious strife that is growing stronger in Kiev around the issue of churches not yet returned to believers by the state. By the way, the Jews are to be given back their ancient synagogue, which now houses a puppet theater.

Many writers, editors and scholars are leaving the Communist party. At the Dnipro publishing house, 14 communists have left; at the journal *Vsesvit* (Universe), virtually all but the editor-in-chief are gone. I think that in September, when everyone comes back from holiday, this process will intensify. At my institute there is no particular movement—there are 75 communists!

But totalitarian thinking is not to be shaken off lightly. One venerable literary elder of advanced years said that writers should leave the CPSU en masse and that they should be forbidden to join other parties. Anyone who joins another party should be ejected from the Writers' Union. He did not say who was to decree the prohibition, but, of course, there is to be someone who would enforce it. He himself is still a party member. He is waiting for the order of the day for a collective exit from the party.

August 19

Today is the Feast of the Transfiguration, and finally it has grown cooler. Before this religious holiday, the Ukrainian Autocephalous Orthodox church was formally registered, as I heard from Maksym Strikha. There was a meeting at St. Sophia's Square organized by the Autocephalous community and the Peasant party. Yesterday physicians' meetings were held throughout the USSR. In Donetsk there were slogans such as "CPSU! Share your wealth with poor medicine!" and a couple of blue-and-yellow flags. But you can no longer impress anyone with meetings. I think the authorities have become used to them. But the physicians are threatening a strike. Somehow I can't square this with the Hippocratic oath, although our pharmacists have long been "on strike." There is not even aspirin to be had in the stores. It's the same throughout the Soviet Union.

August 20

Our academicians Dzeverin and Novychenko, dinosaurs of socialist realism, have again distinguished themselves by signing a collective letter against the removal of a number of statues of procommunist activists, including Halan, in Lviv. Of course, the unfortunate Halan's anti-Vatican pamphlets can hardly evoke any sympathy in Lviv, with its Catholic revolution. The letter was published in *Radianska Ukraina*. Today I went to Dnipro Publishers. Everyone was talking about the academicians' "achievement" and making fun of them.

Society is now openly split. I have ended up across the barricade from many former friends and colleagues (of course, I am not alone, nor am I in bad company). Fortunately, these barricades are imaginary, i.e., ideological, but a great many people are already talking about the possibility of a "Romanian variant."

In the last few days Kiev has been visited by a pitiful Soviet-American peace march. They walked before the Supreme Rada with American and official Soviet Ukrainian flags. No one except *Radianska Ukraina* (the communist mouthpiece) noticed their presence.

There's not much more news to add. Moreover, we'll meet in Kiev soon at the big show—the International Congress of Ukrainian Studies.

All the best.

September 12

I haven't written for a long while, because there hasn't been time. Nor have there been any particularly important events in Kiev, unless, of course, you count scholarly conferences, poetry festivals, twin-city days, newspaper festivals, rock concerts and soccer matches. And now huge posters have appeared to advertise an international jousting match in medieval style. I get the impression that everyone is off his rocker in our unhappy land. While the country agonizes, we amuse ourselves, read poetry and sing songs.

But I am taking things too seriously. And as always, I've been irritated for the past while by surrounding conditions. It's like a persistent cold or a chronic allergy. Wherever you look, everything is calculated to complicate and befoul human existence to the maximum. So I'm somewhat irritated, and the people of Kiev, it seems, have reached their limit of stress and nervous exhaustion. Anger is mounting, and it's being fed by the incompetence of the Gorbachev-Ryzhkov government, which is carrying on some kind of obscure polemics, so far restricted to means of transition to a market economy. No one knows when this "transition" is to take place; only the concept itself is being discussed. Now bread is disappearing from the Moscow stores, and this is leading to panic in Kiev as well.

Yesterday on the street I met an acquaintance who teaches at the university. And she said, as if making an offhand comment, "You know, they say there's no bread in Kiev...." I ran into a store in shock. How could I explain to my three-year-old that because perestroika is taking place in the USSR, there won't be any rolls to have with tea? Fortunately, the store looks perfectly normal; it's full of bread, and there's no lineup. Around the corner, though, there is a line for liquor in which dapper intellectuals rub shoulders with rough alcoholics and tramps. I was relieved. But my friend Maksym Strikha, a deputy to the city council, is not relieved. Because the city may panic at any moment, and then the people will rise up and destroy the new democratic city council, as the French toppled the Bastille. And no one will pay any attention to the blue-and-yellow banner on the flagpole. And they will also destroy the Supreme Rada while its members are away on holiday.

True, those holidays are somewhat illusory. Two days ago the opposition began to hold regular meetings in order to draw up an agenda and bills for the coming session. The Union treaty is the subject of all conversations with people close to parliament and government circles. Recently there was a large meeting in Kiev called by the Ukrainian Republican party against the Union treaty. Today on television they showed a meeting organized in Kharkiv by the oblast party committee. On the central square there was a crowd of men in black suits holding Soviet flags. These worthies, of course, support the treaty. This is inscribed on their well-fed physiognomies.

September 16

On September 14 the monument to Lenin in Lviv was taken down. This is the sixteenth city in Western Ukraine to take this step. To the accompaniment of funeral marches, central television commented on this event, calling it an act of vandalism and a crime against culture. The newspapers are full of polemics concerning monuments to Lenin, but the urge to overthrow the chief is reaching Kiev as well. We are about ten months behind Lviv in the development of the revolutionary process, so that by springtime, according to the logic of history, we should also have one less Lenin.[41] On Khreshchatyk, as you probably remember, there are actually two of them. At least city council has taken a step in this direction: October Revolution Square was renamed Independence Square a few days ago. True, there is no independence as yet, but at least we already have the square.

Soon it will be impossible to find any street in Kiev. The new city council is taking obvious delight in wiping the names of party activists and revolutionaries off the city map. The square named after Lenin's comrade, Uritsky, which became Brezhnev Square for a couple of years, is now called Sinna ploshcha (Hay Square). Kirov Street will probably soon become Hrushevsky Street. They don't know what to do with Heroes of the Revolution Street. At one time it was called Victims of the Revolution Street, but in the 70s, or earlier, the party authorities caught on that the name had a double meaning, so Heroes of the Revolution Street made its appearance. Wags now propose calling it Victims of the Heroes of the Revolution Street.

Big meetings are coming up. At the end of September the Shevchenko Ukrainian Language Society will hold its convention, followed in October by the Rukh congress and the founding conventions of the Democratic party and the Liberal-Democratic party. There are also plans for the convention of a new party that emerged out of the "democratic platform of the CPSU." At least its members requested that communists who remain in the party "not count themselves adherents of the democratic platform." Only those who have broken their ties with the CPSU may join. A few days ago the newspapers said that approximately 50,000 members have left the CPU since the beginning of the year, with about three million remaining. No comment required, as they say. Even though everyone is predicting further defections from the CPSU, its demise is still far off.

The official press does not really report what is going on in the other parties. One can glean something only from *Vechirnii Kyiv* and the unofficial papers.

Aside from party activity, some approximation of normal life, with its own dramas and developments, is still going on in Kiev. Yesterday my sister called me in a panic. Sasha the hairdresser—not only a hairdresser, but a close friend of ours, who has been doing our hair for many years—is leaving for Israel. Sasha is Kiev's best known and most expensive hairdresser, a true aesthete, an artist who never settles for second best and never listens to you, but always knows best what hairdo you need at any given time. For many years he dreamed of having a private salon, while making do with a hairdresser's shop that was actually private but semi-underground. The shop was in a rented room in a dirty working-class residence—a men's residence, at that. Sasha's shop could serve as a marvelous exemplar of our country's social disparities. Here was a run-down, ramshackle residence where you could always find half-drunk, semi-conscious and unbelievably pitiful men. The building was visited by imposing women who would either walk in or drive up in their cars. Among them were actresses, Intourist guides, wives of underground millionaires, and even your humble servant. And so, in the sixth year of perestroika, our Sasha has lost hope of ever having a luxurious salon in Kiev. He is taking his wife and two small children and going to a country where he has no relatives or close friends; he is prepared to live in the desert, even to fight the Iraqis, so as not to remain here. And so the last remaining Jewish family that I know is leaving; the others left long ago. Moreover, this is a professional whose intuition tells him that there is nothing to hope for in this country. And that factor is especially telling.

September 20

A few days ago the newspaper *Komsomolskaia Pravda* published Aleksandr Solzhenitsyn's long article, "Kak nam obustroit' Rossiiu" (How are We to Organize Russia?) On the same day the editor-in-chief of the newspaper gave an interview on the main Soviet television news program, saying that at last the great Russian writer had spoken his great prophetic word. You yourself know how strong the cult of Solzhenitsyn is among us, and you can imagine how everyone rushed to read his article. And now imagine my shock, and that of thousands of others in Ukraine, when we read that Russia is Russia plus Ukraine and Belorussia; that every republic has the right to secede from the Union except Ukraine and Belorussia.

The article is divided into sections. One of them is "A Word to the Ukrainians and Belorussians." It is difficult to render the contents of this "word" and evaluate it as a whole, but it is suffused with one main idea: Ukrainians are part of the Russian people; Ukraine is part of Russia; it turns out that Alexander II's suppression of Ukrainian identity "did not last long" and prepared the "fall of the Russian state structure" (and thus, in the broad historical sense, was even positive); finally the revolution—the "ramshackle socialist Rada of 1917 was brought about by an agreement among politicians, and was not elected by the people"; even the language of Western Ukraine is a patois of Ukrainian, Polish and German words. Furthermore, "to give away Ukraine today" (What an imperialist phrase, "to give away," meaning that they did take it after all) "means cutting through millions of families and people."

So the "great" Russian classic declares, "This cruel separation is unnecessary!"

Further on, Solzhenitsyn makes a pathetic, almost Biblical declaration that our common enemy is communism and explains how we are to fight it. It is difficult to take all this calmly, just as it is impossible to be blasé about one's disappointment in earlier enthusiasms. I remember how, more than ten years ago, as a student and graduate in the Brezhnev period I secretly read Solzhenitsyn in English, because the Russian text was unavailable; how enthusiastic I was about him, as were many of my contemporaries; how I found a picture of him in some issue of *Time* and studied it closely; how I began to read *The GULAG Archipelago* last year in official Russian journals, along with everyone else. But this is a strange time in which everyone is appearing as he really is and cannot hide behind anyone else's mask. Solzhenitsyn, too, has made his position perfectly clear. And this has led to a resurgence of my old pessimistic thoughts—how difficult, how hopelessly difficult it will be for Ukraine to tear itself away from this last empire, when even the empire's most intelligent representatives cannot reconcile themselves to it. I know that there have already been protests from Ukraine to *Komsomolskaia Pravda*; D[mytro] P[avlychko] gave an interview to some foreign journalists, and Roman Lubkivsky—as I heard from my mother, who has just come back from Lviv—has simply fallen ill out of disillusionment.

Like other cities in Ukraine, Kiev is on the verge of starvation. This has never happened before. It is hard to understand where all the food has gone, including rice and pasta; where the gas has gone. There are rumors of sabotage, of a partocratic conspiracy, of buried sausage and meat. I don't know how much of this is to be believed. It is difficult to grasp to what extent the Ukrainian and all-Union authorities comprehend this catastrophic situation. As if anticipating that the people's rage will soon spill out onto the streets, the Presidium of the Ukrainian Supreme Rada decided a few days ago to prohibit all demonstrations in front of its building for a distance of 1,000 meters. The Narodna Rada drew up a protest.

Both sides are preparing for a sharp struggle that will commence in only ten days.

On September 27 the Inter-party Assembly (yet another political bloc of the most radical and implacable) is planning to hold an all-Ukrainian strike. I do not know how successful it will be, but the strike is being openly debated. Television news carries reports about it, showing interviews with people on the streets of Kiev. When asked whether a strike is necessary, most people ask the reporter to go into any store and then to pose his question. The main demands of the strike are to enshrine the Declaration of Sovereignty in Ukraine's constitution, to close the Chernobyl nuclear station immediately, and to recall all citizens of Ukraine from the Red Army if they are not serving on their own territory.

In the middle of all of this, I am now preparing a Ukrainian edition of Emily Dickinson's poems with a group of colleagues. Our publishing houses have less and less paper. Moscow simply refuses to give it to us. We have little of our own. I do not know whether our book will be published at all, or who will read love poetry in a time of hunger. But someone has to take care of such "unimportant" matters. I wrote an introduction and notes to the poems, which our best translators have rendered on the basis of my literal versions. Now I am comparing the translations with the originals.

Of course, I also attend meetings on occasion. They take place almost every Sunday, and many of my friends, most of whom are now involved in politics, are trying mightily to involve me in some new party or organization. This is especially true of those who are organizing the Democratic party. I have even been invited to the party's regional conference in Terebovlia (a city in the Ternopil region where the Democratic party has a very large following). I am resisting with all my strength; I remain an ordinary Rukh member in the Institute of Literature.

September 22

Yesterday Gorbachev spoke at the USSR Supreme Soviet and the speech was shown on the main USSR news program. Although I found it irritating, I heard him out to the end. It was the same thing again: the transition to the market. As always, in the course of speaking the general secretary got all fired up, even excited, and sharply criticized the republics' declarations of sovereignty. He made it very clear that for him and the "center" these declarations were meaningless. He said that it was time for the "euphoria of declarations" to end and for everyone to get to work. And anyone who encouraged peoples to claim independence and separate was a political adventurist. Moreover, he demanded that the Supreme Soviet grant him extraordinary powers that are supposedly required for the transition to the market, including the introduction of direct presidential rule over the republics and the dissolution of their parliaments. This is becoming a bit frightening, disturbing people here in Kiev. Mind you, the RSFSR Supreme Soviet announced today that such powers for Gorbachev are inadmissible.

Some liberal central newspapers hint that the "center" has itself become a province; that the USSR as a state no longer exists. The formulation is interesting, but only theoretically true. However, things have become easier in a sense. My neighbor, the choreographer of our Opera Theater, told me yesterday that there probably will be no military coup. This is what two women—a literary scholar and a choreographer—talk about when they meet in Kiev! For several years now, any conversation here has led quickly to the question of whether there will be a military coup or not. Now it is said that the military has lost its chance or its historic opportunity to turn back the clock. There is tremendous opposition to the Soviet army. It seems that the struggle for the creation of a national army or, at least, not to release soldiers from Ukraine is becoming the most unifying idea among us. It unites people even more than the ecological question.

September 26

It seems that my optimism of two days ago was premature, for today's news is not encouraging. The all-Ukrainian strike has been postponed to October 1. This confusion over the date is a major political error. As always, no one here knows what is to happen where and when. And this is leading to feelings verging on panic. Rukh is planning a demonstration in Kiev on September 30 that is to be attended by about a million people. On the following day there is to be a strike and a march along both sides of the Dnieper, i.e., from both sides of Kiev to the Supreme Rada. This is being organized by the Inter-party Assembly. It is forecast that 30% of Kiev's enterprises intend to strike (I have this figure from city council).

According to the organizers of both actions, thousands of people from all over Ukraine are to arrive. Larysa Skoryk, who spoke a few days ago at a meeting of the oblast council in Lviv, said that a blockade of Kiev is being prepared in order to prevent buses from coming through. But there is an even more unpleasant item of news. Beginning tomorrow, on the orders of General Gromov, a state of battle-readiness is being introduced in Kiev, and on the 29th and 30th military maneuvers will take place in the Kiev military district. I learned this two hours ago from Maksym Strikha when he brought me the latest batch of his translations of Emily Dickinson. His mood was very pessimistic. Today the leaders of the strike committees came to the city council, very firm of purpose. The military is also very determined, and so the unpredictable may happen. Tensions are rising in Kiev. An hour ago—it's nighttime now—a friend who is far removed from politics called me to say that the city is abuzz and asked me, as a person who frequents political circles, what will happen tomorrow. As far as I know, nothing will happen tomorrow. But a great deal will be happening on the weekend. On the 29th, besides the convention of the Language Society, the Memorial Society is holding a large forum; there is also the day of remembrance and sorrow for the victims of Babyn Yar, which will also bring out a mass of people.

1. Miners from Donetsk demonstrating in Kiev, autumn 1990. (*Iefrem Lukatsky*)

2. Miners picket parliament, autumn 1990. The sign reads, "Enough empty chatter and useless ideas." (*Serhii Supinsky*)

3. Miners picket parliament, autumn 1990. (*Iefrem Lukatsky*)

4. Committee of Mothers of Soldiers before the parliament building, autumn 1990. (*Pavlo Pashchenko*)

5. On Khreshchatyk in front of the Central Department Store. (*Serhii Supinsky*)

6. On Khreshchatyk, Red Army Day, May 9, 1990. (*Serhii Supinsky*)

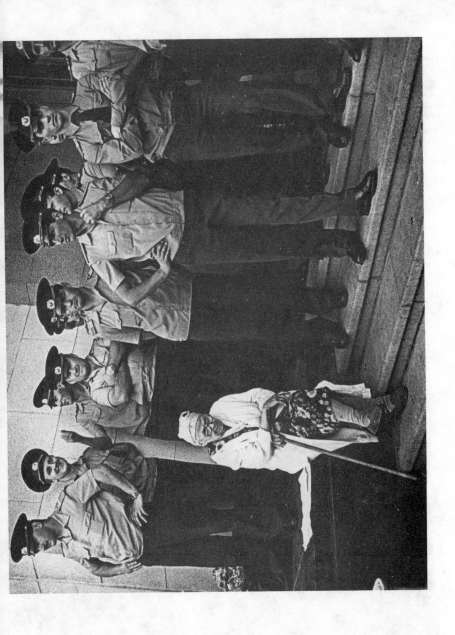

7. Police gather on Khreshchatyk, autumn 1990. (*Pavlo Pashchenko*)

8. Student strikers with banners demanding abolition of military draft and the formation of a professional Ukrainian national army, October 1990. (*Iefrem Lukatsky*)

9. Student hunger strike camp on October Revolution Square with banner, "Out with the traitors to the Ukrainian people—Kravchuk and Company," October 1990. (*Serhii Supinsky*)

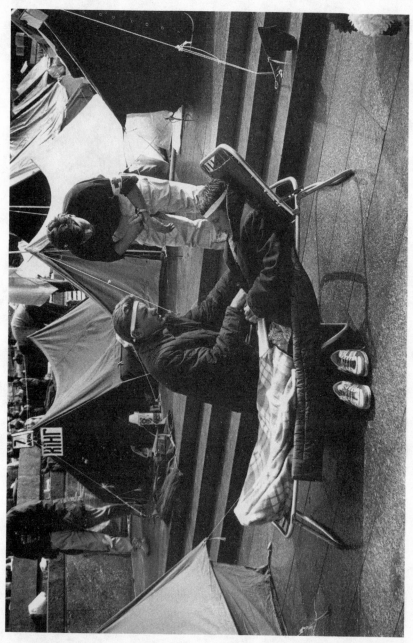

10. The Kiev Institute of the National Economy contingent at the student hunger strike camp on October Revolution Square (now Independence Square), October 1990. (*Serhii Supinsky*)

11. Meeting on October Revolution Square (now Independence Square), October 1990. (*Serhii Supinsky*)

12. The student hunger strike ends, October 1990. (*Serhii Supinsky*)

13. Picket near St. Sophia Cathedral blocking the arrival of the Moscow Patriarch, Aleksii, October 29, 1990. (*Pavlo Pashchenko*)

14. Demonstrators protesting the arrival of the Moscow Patriarch, Aleksii, near St. Sophia Cathedral, October 29, 1990. (*Pavlo Pashchenko*)

15. Parliamentary session. Communist deputies stand in protest. (*Slavko Maievsky*)

16. Parliamentary session. Communist deputies (*left*) confront deputies from Lviv (*right*). (*Slavko Maievsky*)

September 27

As I expected, things are quiet today in Kiev. But tension continues to build. The head of the Kiev police made an appearance on the evening news and announced that the political demonstration planned by Rukh for September 30 is sanctioned by city council, but the demonstration planned for October 1 before the parliament building is not permitted and has no sanction. The police are therefore calling upon Kievans not to go out onto the streets, and promises to apply appropriate measures. So they will disperse the demonstration! Moreover, all of Kiev is being dug up: all the roads and streets near the Supreme Rada seem to be in need of repair. Also, roadblocks are being set up on the city's perimeter so as not to let anyone into the city.

Today *Literaturna Ukraina* printed an appeal from the Narodna Rada asking citizens to come to parliament on October 1. This creates the potential for the completely unforeseeable, and once again everyone is actively discussing the possibilities of a coup. There is a chance that the disorder will provoke Gorbachev to dissolve parliament and introduce presidential rule in Ukraine. This is the least pleasant possibility. One wants to be optimistic, but it is difficult to shake dark thoughts. April 1989 in Tbilisi is too fresh in the memory. There is even an anecdote making the rounds in Kiev: "The members of parliament arrive on October 1, and men in military uniforms tell them, "Citizen members of parliament, this is the wrong entrance; off you go to the buses with window grates." I don't want to end on this note, because I cannot and do not wish to expect the worst, but there is no help for it. That's my mood today.

I expect things are normal with you. Probably there will soon be snow and you will start to go skiing in the mountains. Even now, I long for calm, quiet Edmonton; I think of the mountains and the prairies.

September 30 - October 11

It looks as if our political season has started—energetically, incisively, and with a promise of scandal.

For a week before the opening of the second session of parliament, the atmosphere in Kiev had been oppressive. On Friday, September 28, the Presidium of the Supreme Rada published an appeal to the people. Words to the effect that there is no point in drafting a new Union treaty before Ukraine adopts its constitution. On Friday night the city executive committee finally sanctioned the demonstration set for the first of October. On Friday the Plenum of the Central Committee of the CPU at last took place and Kravchuk prudently stepped down as the secretary of the Central Committee.

Finally, Friday was Dmytro Pavlychko's birthday. We didn't invite anyone because D[mytro] P[avlychko] was busy preparing his speech for the conference of the Ukrainian Language Society, which was to begin the next day. In fact, he didn't come home until late in the evening. Meanwhile Roman Lubkivsky showed up, as did one of mother's friends and my parents' friend from Toronto, Askold Hankivsky. We waited and waited, then started on the scotch, then the food, then who should show up but D[mytro] P[avlychko] with Roman Ivanychuk. (Having become the director of a parliamentary subcommission, Ivanychuk has settled in that dreadful hotel you know too well, the Moskva, where everything is crumbling and falling down irrevocably, it seems.) And this modest little family gathering, which included three deputies, sat several hours around the table in an extraordinarily cheerful mood. We laughed without a break, told various stories about parliamentary life—for example, how admirers sometimes mistake Ivanychuk for Khmara on the street—and other kinds of incidents. We conjectured who of the deputies—when it comes to that—will crawl upon the high dome of the parliament to plant the blue-and-yellow flag. And so on.

The next day, September 29, the conference of the Language Society opened at the October Palace of Culture. Everything proceeded in a very businesslike manner without that exaltation and intensity which were evident a year ago. However, there were still a lot of rambling speeches made up of literary quotations. Everyone had a good laugh at the representative of the Ukrainian Cossack Brotherhood—there is such a thing. A young man in a Cossack jacket, voluminous trousers and a prop sword said that Ukrainians need not refer to Western social experience but need only revive the free Cossack republic and its main idea of the freedom of the individual. But D[mytro] P[avlychko] gently persuaded this Cossack-anarchist to remove himself, for he had burst onto the stage quite out of order. Even so, there were some who vigorously applauded him. The next day Pavlo Movchan was elected head of the society.

The solemn requiem assembly at Babyn Yar on September 30 was an exceptionally moving event of major significance. Many people attended and everyone, not just the Jews, wept for the victims executed 49 years ago.

That same day the congress of the Greens wound up; they finally founded their party and chose Yurii Shcherbak[42] as leader. Later that same day they formed up at the meeting in highly disciplined ranks, carrying their green flags and green tridents.

But the most important event of the day was a meeting and demonstration the likes of which Kiev has never seen. The meeting opened at three o'clock near Central Stadium. It began despite the fact that all the roads into Kiev had been closed, with armored cars at the approaches to the city on the pretext that the soldiers in these military vehicles had come to collect the harvest. Ten huge army trucks were positioned on Repin, my street, alone. People arrived from all over Ukraine. Among others, the poet Liuba Holota had flown in the day before from Dnipropetrovsk and saw for herself how the plane was loaded up with German shepherd police dogs, allegedly on their way to a dog show in Kiev.

But back to the meeting. On the square there must have been several hundred blue-and-yellow and red-and-black flags. At the demonstration itself there were thousands. All the important political figures spoke—Larysa Skoryk, Levko

Lukianenko, Serhii Holovaty, Volodymyr Yavorivsky, D[mytro] P[avlychko] (whom *Pravda* sarcastically lampooned that day for having called for the establishment of a national army), Pavlo Movchan, Yurii Shcherbak, Stepan Khmara, the leaders of all the major parties except the CPU, representatives of the committee of soldiers' mothers, of the Union of Ukrainian Women, of the oblasts, and so on. The main theme was the rejection of the Union treaty in any form.

People are so excited and so subject to the authority of their leaders that they are prepared to accept even contradictory summonses from them. Someone said: "Russia is the same kind of empire as the USSR. No contact with Russia is possible!" Applause. Following a couple of speeches, D[mytro] P[avlychko] said: "We're for a democratic Russia, for new relations with her as with an independent state!" More applause.

At 5:00 p.m. a protest march departed from the stadium along Red Army and Khreshchatyk streets. At least 200,000 (and perhaps 500,000) people in enormously wide, tightly packed columns, singing and yelling slogans—"Freedom for Ukraine!" "Out with Masol and Kravchuk!" "No Union treaty!" "Down with the CPU!"—moved out onto Lenin Komsomol Square. The column came to a halt near the two monuments of Lenin and people began chanting, "Down with the idol!" Near one of the monuments a ring of defenders took up their positions, among them decorated veterans and, probably, KGB men in disguise. Foreign television correspondents paced about. Police stood in ranks around the second Lenin statue which, in April, had been decorated with a wreath of barbed wire.

When they walked past the City Soviet, deputies holding blue-and-yellow flags appeared in the windows. Among them I recognized Maksym Strikha, the tallest of the lot.

People stood on all the balconies along the route. Most of them waved their hands or even flags. The crowd stuck to the sidewalks; some joined up with the marchers, others looked on anxiously. I saw a former university teacher of mine there. He used to come with us students when we went out to do involuntary labor on the collective farms, and drove us like a fiend. He was the secretary of the communist party organization and directed it just as ferociously. He was looking at the column utterly terrified.

It's difficult to describe my feelings—the feelings of a person who walked in this column—just as it's difficult even approximately to describe the panorama of a sea of flags and excited people. At the meeting, I met Ihor Rymaruk with his friends, who had come from Ternopil expressly for this action. I walked on with them, seeing dozens of other people I knew. It was full of people like me, not at all populists, but complete aesthetes, various exotic types with long hair or ponytails—rock musicians, film directors, poets, hippies, that is, all those to whom even six months ago every sort of "national idea" seemed alien. As for taking part in some demonstration, it would have seemed a totally unnatural act! We made it to the end of Khreshchatyk by about seven in the evening. My feet felt battered and burned up from the long hours of standing and walking; my head was buzzing from all the shouting and slogans. Yet we could barely drag ourselves away (not even wanting to go home) and agreed to meet up the next day near the Supreme Rada.

First of October: a day of strikes and one more demonstration. The movement of people in Kiev began very early in the morning. It was singing that woke me up—a column of strikers singing on their way to the center. From there organized columns proceeded up Kirov Street to the Supreme Rada, from there again along Khreshchatyk and then back where they started. According to our newspapers, 120,000-150,000 people marched in the columns. They formed up the first circle at ten o'clock, but the second didn't work out. They got jammed up near the Supreme Rada. At about noon deputies from the Narodna Rada came out into the square, for by that time a scandal had already broken out and the democratic bloc, comprising 146 deputies, had left the hall.

The first scandal happened during the opening minutes of the session. Kravchuk had just come up to the podium to make a statement about the agenda when Porovsky, Movchan and other deputies of the Narodna Rada showed up in the hall with a blue-and-yellow flag. All jumped up from their seats, and some partocrats rushed to seize the flag. It was virtually a brawl. Journalists with cameras slipped into the very thick of the brouhaha, while Kravchuk stood at the podium and yelled at the opposition to restore order. There was an unbelievable roar. The pushing and shoving was thoroughly unparliamentary, but finally peace was somehow restored and the flag put away, although little flags did turn up on the desks of the democratic bloc. And Mykhailo Horyn, looking exhausted and weary, mainly just sat—in a silk tie with blue and yellow stripes, our national colors.

When the first scandal had somehow been brought under control, and Pliushch had taken away the flag, Kravchuk delivered his proposals and also declared that no consolidation with the opposition was possible. He cited an article by Levko Lukianenko and announced that Levko was summoning the people to an adventure of the Romanian sort. Such aggressiveness from Kravchuk heated up the already testy atmosphere in the hall. Next, Yukhnovsky spoke for the opposition, declaring that the empire ought to disintegrate, and proceeded to read the proposals of the Narodna Rada in this regard.

Lukianenko declared that the resolution of the presidium of the Supreme Rada of September 26—that it is forbidden to stand in the square while parliament is in session—was unconstitutional. At this point Kravchuk put the question to a vote, and 263 deputies voted *for* sustaining the resolution, that is, *for* the prohibition of meetings in the square!

But the scandal that forced the democrats out of the hall began after Serhii Konev's speech. He read out the Declaration of the Association of Democratic Assemblies of Ukraine, which concludes with a call for the dissolution of the powerless parliament. Noise and shouts. Repeating the words, "Kravchuk has wrecked the session! Kravchuk has wrecked the session!", Khmara materialized on the podium, and then Kravchuk declared a break. The meeting had lasted barely an hour and a half.

At that point I was standing in the square before parliament with the same bohemian gang of the day before, photographing the banners. People were singing a new song: "Kravchuk baby, Kravchuk baby, fly, fly like a little bird—to Moscow and Ivashko!" Then a meeting began, with speeches by deputies of the opposition—the Narodna Rada. We shifted a little to the sidelines, for, squeezed between the fence to the rear and the police at the front, we found it somewhat frightening to keep standing in that jam-packed crowd. The crowd had a varied profile, from the most radical, who demanded the dissolution of parliament, to the most sober-minded, who feared a constitutional crisis and the onset of presidential rule. Police wandered about in the crowd, reading the slogans. Some with evident satisfaction, others with horror. The whole park around the Supreme Rada was overrun with OMON (riot control police). Dressed in bullet-proof vests and helmets, they have become a routine sight in our streets.

The next meeting of parliament began at four o'clock. Les Taniuk read out a declaration on behalf of the Narodna Rada demanding the resignation of the chairman and the prime minister and the retraction of the resolution of September 26. Then Filenko, a member of the Democratic Platform, criticized extremists of the right and left, but also demanded the resignation of Kravchuk and Masol. Then Kotsiuba, the former opposition deputy, spoke, definitively exposing himself as a traitor in his support of the government in unison with Hurenko. During the break, Kravchuk deliberated with the representatives of the strike committees. Under pressure from him, the deputies announced themselves in favor of permitting a representative of the strike committees to present their demands.

The committee co-ordinator, Mykhailo Ratushny, spoke. In a threatening voice he read out the text that was hanging on every post and pole in Kiev, and gave the government one month to meet their demands. On this note the first day ended. That evening it was reported on the news that the strike had failed, although it was not clear how many enterprises in Kiev struck. However, this same newscast hinted that the majority had supported the strikers' demands. The exact number of those who participated in the strike is unknown, although in Kiev several large factories as well as some individual shops went on strike.

October 2

Just as everybody foresaw, there was a fight outside the Supreme Rada between some of the demonstrators—almost 2,000 of them—and detachments of the riot control police. There are injured on both sides. All of this raised a great ruckus and commotion in parliament while deputies ran from the parliament building onto the square to try to calm the crowd. Then an investigative commission was struck. Yemets, the chair of the human rights commission, addressed parliament with an appeal that it abrogate its decision to forbid people from congregating in the square. In vain.

So, there are some 30 victims of the battlefield and there is the unbelievable stubbornness of the parliamentary majority, the communists, who do not want to permit people to stand about in the square and unceasingly, doggedly shout the same word at them over and over: "Shame!"

On the same day at another square—near the "idol," as it is now referred to—that is, on Khreshchatyk not far from Lenin, the students have begun a hunger strike. There are 138 of them. They've erected tents on the pavement and they lie on cheap, thin blankets with headbands that say, "I am on hunger strike." There's no deadline to this strike, but it's calculated to last two weeks, after which the strikers will be replaced by new ones.

The tent site is attracting lots of attention as the first sight of its kind in Kiev. The corpulent and well-fed police stand over them—they're protecting the monument to Lenin, the idol of our system. The biggest change altogether in the Kiev landscape is the incredible number of police. Not far from home, near the older Lenin monument, there is a police car constantly on watch and almost a whole battalion of police standing about. My three-and-a-half-year-old daughter finds this exciting to see. She yells down the whole street so that the police themselves can hear her: "Mummy, mummy, look! Police! What are they doing?" Just try to explain to her what they are doing.

The leader of the opposition, Yukhnovsky, visited the hunger strikers. Interviewed on television, he said that, at a time of struggle for independence, such actions are justifiable. On Friday, the 5th, Kravchuk showed up to try to persuade the students to stop the strike, promising to look into all their demands. Among these demands is the dismissal of Prime Minister Masol, the nationalization of party property, the recall of Ukrainian citizens serving in the Soviet Army outside Ukraine, the renunciation of the proposed Union treaty and, finally, the least realistic demand of all—the dissolution of parliament and new elections for the following spring.

But the leadership of the CP is trying somehow to counter the students. On Saturday, the 6th, at the Ukraine Palace, on Red Army Street, a congress of veterans took place for which the party mobilized its finest old stalwarts. Afterwards, these 500 geezers and grannies proceeded, with red flags and portraits of Lenin, several kilometers to the square where the students are on hunger strike. The authorities had earlier driven a brass band to the square in order to accompany the laying of wreaths. But, to the great delight of the striking students and the crowd, the orchestra, which had been waiting a long time while the old folks hobbled their way up to the Lenin monument, struck up a funeral march at the appropriate moment. This produced a quite fantastic exhilaration among the students and their sympathizers.

For some time people in Kiev had known and spoken about the preparations for this demonstration of the "politically deceased," and so some deputies (among them D[mytro] P[avlychko]) had come to the square beforehand to prevent any kind of clash. But everything passed peacefully. People in the crowd bearing the blue-and-yellow flags silently waved their hands at those bearing the red. The young people roared with laughter.

True, the all-Union evening television program, *Vremia* (Time), reported triumphantly on the "many thousands" present at the Kiev gathering (there weren't even a thousand).

On the next day, Sunday the 7th, a small gang of literary types, myself included, made our way across the yard in early morning to the tent city and found ourselves a place near the banner, "Ukrainian writers in solidarity with Ukrainian students." Our group consisted of young poets, various sorts of avant-gardists and literary hooligans (actually they're serious writers, but some older literary retrogrades and socialist realists consider them to be hooligans) gathered and grouped together by Ihor Rymaruk.

The sensations were altogether strange. We sat behind a virtually imaginary barrier marked by a rope strung around the tent city. Beyond this rope the crowd was pushed together as though in a zoo. Within the perimeter of the rope were the students on hunger strike, other students looking after the camp and keeping order, journalists, priests, and various groups of supporters. One rather well-known poet stood for many hours behind the rope but never took the risk of joining us. He explained that he had problems at work and didn't want to be hung with the label, "He was there as well." Such ambivalence in our time, when it is simply absurd to think of patching up our society, when one wants simply to sweep it away, to destroy it, leaves me feeling very depressed.

Thus the crowd looked at us, we looked at the crowd— between us was the rope barrier, which served as an invisible barricade—and listened to the debates of the onlookers. Some scolded the layabouts, others passed flowers across the rope, still others said that it wouldn't make any difference, and why were they wrecking their health? (A few days ago, I rode by on the trolley and heard one old woman in an odious red wig, with honorific ribbons all over her chest, say, "Trash! Bums! They should be bringing in the harvest on the collective farms.") However, those who brought flowers as a sign of their sympathy were many times more numerous. You had the feeling, from those countless bouquets, that you were sitting at some large graveside. But most numerous of all were those who watched in silence, not understanding what was happening here and why. However, it was obvious from the strained faces that people were considering: if there are those who are sacrificing themselves for the sake of some list of five political demands, maybe there is something serious behind it.

We spoke with some students who were still in good shape. Those who had been fasting for seven days were already dreadfully weakened. Of the 138 who had begun, only 87 were left on the Sunday. Some had ended up in hospital. In fact, someone or other was brought there daily. Among the strikers were Russian anarchists from Irkutsk and a young woman from Azerbaidzhan who had married a Ukrainian.

Together with a Canadian journalist looking for someone to interview, we approached a twenty-two-year-old boy from Lviv who was sitting by his tent and strumming something on his guitar. And here he told us that his parents had died of hard work—his mother had been a dairymaid on a collective farm and his father had been invalided from a factory. He had been left quite alone and thus could give his life for the freedom of Ukraine, not causing anyone close to him any grief. He said this very calmly, without vehemence, as if making a chance remark, all the while plucking at his guitar.

He made a staggering impression on me. Hardly ten years younger than I, he was like a person from another world, with notions quite different from those of the students with whom I had studied. Oksana Zabuzhko, who was also there, commented on this as a sign of the birth of a new generation which has very little in common with the wasted and mutilated feeling of emptiness and futility with which we lived during our student years a decade ago.

It's terrible that with every passing day one more hunger striker ends up in the resuscitation unit. Nevertheless their number keeps growing, more and more new students join up; and on the 10th of October, disappointed with the way the session was going, eight parliamentary deputies announced their intention to go on hunger strike too. On the evening of the 10th, on Khreshchatyk, spontaneous and highly extraordinary events took place. But first, something about what caused them.

From the very beginning, parliament had begun to spin its wheels on every question that was presented, whether amendments to our Brezhnevite and nugatory constitution fit for nothing but the garbage heap, or government efforts to stabilize the economy, or Ukrainian citizens' service in the Soviet army. These are all key questions, very important in the sense of a further distancing from the Union, which some dream of and others fear. That's why the struggle started off so frenzied and persistent.

At the parliamentary session of October 3 there was a whiff of the government's impending resignation. Its proposals for the stabilization of the economic situation in the republic brought together the "right" and the "left." All spoke against it. The government's plan appeared so ineffectual (among other things it provided for the transfer of 39% of hard-currency earnings to the all-Union budget) that the question of non-confidence in it and of the resignation of Prime Minister Masol, whom two days ago the slogan-shouters in the square were calling "Masolini," was raised. Masol wasn't there and the question was tabled until October 8 with the apparent intention of conducting a vote of non-confidence in the government. But after a few days the bloc of 239 reconsidered the situation and, making use of their majority, rescued Masol.

The other question that was discussed was that of the army. Moscow has ignored all the resolutions from Ukraine about the recall of Ukrainian citizens from the Soviet army and about service on its own territory. In the meantime, deserters who have been beaten and maimed by their officers or by their own comrades have fled and are hiding out at home or in western Ukraine. Our new women's organizations are involved in transferring them and giving them sanctuary. Can you imagine what this is we've come to? The Writers' Union of Ukraine has now become the headquarters of the Organization of Soldiers' Mothers, which is demanding radical decisions about the army. The parliament is incapable of such drastic resolution. It adopted a motion about future service on Ukrainian territory, but this does not include those who are already in the army.

The writer Maria Vlad, an activist in the women's movement, related a horrifying story of how, a couple of days ago, two Russian boys—not from Ukraine but from Russia itself— came to the Union. They had been horribly abused and, having learned that the Writers' Union might give them protection, made their way here after travelling illegally thousands of kilometers from Siberia, penniless, hungry, in tatters, and asked for help. They were given a change of clothes and directed to western Ukraine.

At last the democrats have made an attempt to confer constitutional validity on the Declaration of Sovereignty. The partocrats sank the idea, and sank another, far more moderate, project for the ratification of all-Union laws by the Parliament of Ukraine.

Thus, the fact that Masol did not lose his post; that all its decisions appear retrograde; and that the opposition is powerless to influence the majority, which ignores common sense, resulted in the crowd's spontaneously blocking off Khreshchatyk and stopping traffic. The entire opposition—the Narodna Rada—came to the students on the square, where they had a spontaneous meeting. Then some of the deputies together with the crowd went off to take the television station by storm in order to go live on air with an appeal to the people. By late evening they had managed it, and Yemets, Khmara and others spoke on television. Then Kravchuk arrived at the station and very late at night also addressed the people. A funny thing happened. Kravchuk was sitting beside Okhmakevych, chairman of the State Committee on Television, and asked him: "Have I prohibited you from letting deputies appear on television?" And Okhmakevych answered, "No, Leonid Makarovych, you haven't forbidden it."

That's what we've come to. Total agony. The public is agitated in the extreme. Hatred toward the authorities increases. The hunger strike is expanding, parliamentarians storm the t.v. station. Groups of young people—very young boys and girls—roam the streets shouting, "Freedom for Ukraine!" Marvelous Ukrainian women clandestinely arrange for the transfer of army deserters to western Ukraine. I simply can't imagine what is going to happen next. In this sense, everything remains as before. Just as it was a year or two ago, the situation is unforeseen and unpredictable.

When we met in Kiev, you said to me: "Write something about your own life as well." This provoked an interesting thought in me: that I should at least think, if not write, about my everyday life.

I've thought a lot about this and come to the conclusion that, during these last years, it has become stranger and stranger, even absurd. What kind of life is it, anyway? I show up at work twice a week, and almost every time, having arrived at the institute, I ask myself why I've bothered. Rambling along the corridors from coffee to coffee are these guys, my colleagues, who haven't done anything for decades and who are protected by our labor laws and our pseudo-liberal bosses. You don't see those who are actually working, because they are in the libraries or at home. Even though each department might wish it, it's impossible to work at our workplaces, and each department has no fewer than ten staffers, with one room for all of them, crowded with tables.

So, in our institute you come just to put in an appearance; yet even now our director—for reasons known only to himself—likes to wander through the rooms, making lists of the absentees. He then posts their names on a special board and demands an explanation. As for genuine work, studies, and the quantity and quality of written articles, the bosses don't care. Our director has spent his whole life writing about the positive influence of Lenin's ideas on Soviet literature. For this he was made an Academician. Now that times are changing, he sits drinking cognac under a portrait of Lenin that still hangs in his office, as in all the offices of our bosses at the Academy.

Having taken a turn around the institute and shown everyone that I am still alive, I quietly disappear. My life at home consists in writing and translating from morning to night, metaphorically speaking, for I work mainly at night, my days being taken up with looking after my daughter (our housekeeper left us, and I can't send my daughter to the daycare center because I don't want her speaking that Ukraini-an-Russian patois), chasing down food, cooking, cleaning up, doing the laundry, etc.

I often take the child with me when I rush around to my publishers. I run: this is the most accurate word, for I can't remember when I was last operating in a normal mode. I'm always hurrying, always running, I always have something important to get written by tomorrow, some article to hand in, something to edit, to translate. I sit up till all hours of the night, at eight in the morning my daughter wakes me, I walk around until eleven as though I were still asleep, drinking cup after cup of black tea. And then the cycle begins again.

All my conversations with friends are about politics: all "mundane" outings are to meetings and conferences, to literary or academic gatherings. All the conversations at home or with my parents are also about politics or about the latest literary events.

Among other things, a couple of days ago the first Ukrainian edition of W.B. Yeats was published with my foreword and notes. Naturally, I am very happy. Now I dream about getting Ezra Pound published in Ukrainian. I'm collect-ing material for such an edition. And I want to write a major study about D.H. Lawrence.

A certain apocalyptic mood is very widespread in Kiev, and it's easy enough to explain. In the first place it's connected with Chernobyl. The "sarcophagus" that encloses the damaged block is so full of holes that from time to time it vents radioac-tive dust. This whole structure has somehow or other to be repaired, as *Vechirnii Kyiv* reported openly on October 4. Every second person has radiophobia. I, too, of course. Besides these fears there are other, smaller ones. For example, the fear of falling ill and ending up in hospital. There aren't enough medicines, and there is always the chance you could get infected with AIDS from a dirty syringe. For a whole year I haven't taken my daughter to the doctor, putting off her vaccinations as long as possible for fear of some infection. I was in the grocery today for exactly 10 minutes and overheard so many terrible things that I went about feeling very depressed all day. No one believes in economic improvement. At least I never meet such people. Besides, the fear of radiation is so strong and oppressive that you can subconsciously sense it in others, and this just re-generates apathy. At the same time it frees you from all those other fears which our society has implanted in people's genes.

Nevertheless there are many cautious and prudent people who think that everything can be turned back. Very few people have left the Communist party at Kiev University; at the department where I was a graduate student—Romance and Germanic Languages—no one at all has left, although the party organization has had to disband all the same because absolutely no one agreed to be secretary, which is to say to occupy the post that, five years ago, people were fighting for.

On the way home from work I noticed a sign on the Central department store: "As of October 1, shopping by passport only." That is, in order to buy anything, you have to show your passport with the Kiev registration; if you're from Lviv, say, then no one will sell you anything in Kiev. This system has already existed quite some time in Moscow as a "temporary" measure, but those who dreamed it up have no idea how humiliating and damaging it is to the psyche. I try not to buy anything, but sometimes I ask myself: what if I do need to buy something? At home we haven't had sugar for a whole month, for instance. Sugar is rationed—to buy it you need special "sugar" coupons. But this is to no avail, since it has disappeared from the stores. We don't have coupons either, because the caretaker who is supposed to give them out has also vanished somewhere. I've taught my daughter to drink tea with honey. But how do I explain to Bohdanna, who is three and a half, why there is no sugar or bananas or fish, why in the toy store there are no toys and in the candy store there are no candies....

I'm happy when I can retreat from the world into my computer room and write. However, I recently experienced a real blow in connection with my beloved computer. Dnipro Publishers wouldn't accept my article on Emily Dickinson, which I had printed out beautifully on my printer. They said that the spacing between the letters didn't correspond to the Soviet standard. So I had to take the article to a typist, proofread it once again, and correct the errors.... The same thing with Veselka Publishers. I'm retyping my translation of Peter Shostak's book in the old-fashioned way. It seems that here you still have to pay for civilization. Will things ever change?

Bohdan, please tell me if I am becoming boring and excessively gloomy. It seems to me that lately I have lost my sense of humor. Is that true?

October 18

It's Thursday, the 18th. The middle of the day. I'm at home, sitting at my writing desk, and I can hear an uproar from the festive student demonstration in the square. Theirs is a hard-won victory, and it seems that all of Kiev is celebrating with them today. This is an incredible victory. BBC radio has just called me from London to ask what's going on here and what it means. The meaning of what has happened is difficult to explain in its totality. But a little bit of optimism has suddenly poked up its head. They're folding up their tents on the square, the students are singing and the people of Kiev are calling each other up to offer congratulations on the victory.

The last three days have been full of a drama and tension never before experienced here.

The student strike began on the first of October, as you will recall, and gradually became the central event in our lives. At first, the bureaucrats in parliament laughed at the students and ignored their demands, simply voting not to review them or to review only three of them. Meanwhile, the young people were gaining ground and all of Kiev was waking up little by little. Every day there were more tents. Fortunately, the weather continued to be warm—amazingly, almost like summer weather.

But the nights were cold, naturally, and it was hard—physically and psychologically—in full view of this enormous, yet sluggish and apathetic city, to struggle against a conservative parliament (especially at the beginning, risking life and limb). It's a parliament controlled by the bloc of "239"—"For Soviet Ukraine"—behind which stand Moscow, Gorbachev with his Nobel prize, his enormous army, the KGB, the riot police, and all sorts of veterans with their flapping old men's jowls and their loyalty to "socialist" ideals.

During the hunger strike there was a continual stream of abuse from official Moscow: that there is a "cloud of nationalism hovering over Ukraine" and that "these young people will yet rue their ingloriously lost youth" and, most important, "shame to the political adventurists who stand behind the student extremists." Such was the refrain from the official Moscow newscasts. Borys Oliinyk, in *Pravda*, reproached those who "stand behind the students" and called on communists to not "throw your pearls before swine." At the same time, Russian students were also in the square as a sign of solidarity. (The students have called this square "Sovitska ploshcha" (Soviet square). There is a new fashion among us now, born somewhere in the depths of the Republican party or in the Union of Ukrainian Youth, not to translate into Ukrainian the word "Soviet"—a word introduced from another country by occupiers. Hence "Sovitskyi Soiuz" (Soviet Union), "Sovitska ploshcha," and so on. In other words, it's all foreign, the occupiers', alien.)

But to backtrack a bit. On Saturday evening I got a call from Maksym Strikha (these days the deputies of the municipal executive council ignore weekends and holidays), who informed me that on Monday, the 16th, there was going to be an all-Kiev student strike and a demonstration near the parliament. The Kiev city council has now become transformed into the headquarters of the revolution—they hold meetings at night and then, in their full complement, go on "walkabouts" to prevent citizens' clashes with the police.

On days off, which have become days of expectation, leaflets have appeared in the city: "Citizens of Kiev! Don't let the students on hunger strike die at the hands of the political living dead!" The student strike began on Friday; about a third of Kiev students didn't go to school, and a third represents tens of thousands. But that was only the rehearsal. On Monday you had the impression that no one at all was in school. In the morning a crowd of young people moved onto the square with those same hugely popular slogans of our time: "Freedom for Ukraine!" "Down with the CPU!" and "Out with Masol!" About eleven o'clock I found myself there, near the tent city. Groups of young people were arriving from all directions, some of them just kids—schoolchildren, high-school students. There was a little large measure of surrealism in it—for example, those carrying the red-and-black flag of the Organization of Ukrainian Nationalists and talking among themselves in Russian. Someone at the megaphone announced the names of those educational establishments which were striking. (And the Russian-language remarks of onlookers nearby: "And what's the meaning of these red-and-black flags?") An enormous crowd with the hunger strikers in the first rows—those who could still walk—moved on up to the Supreme Rada. Among them were deputies of the Supreme Rada who had joined the strike on Friday.

The demonstration turned out even bigger than the one for the First of October, and that one had more than 100,000 participants. On this occasion the columns were made up exclusively of youth. I approached the Academy building on Kirov Street, that is, my place of work. Almost all my co-workers had spilled out onto the street to watch the columns of demonstrators. At the same time, in the institute itself, one of the Rukh activists—a wonderful person and a specialist in Russian poetry, Nataliia Mazepa, was collecting signatures in support of the students' demands. Unexpectedly—and this was awful—some refused to sign. Among these "some" were our bosses and some of my former friends and coevals. As to why they refused, I can offer no rational explanation.

So, tens of thousands of students gathered at the Supreme Rada. At this time, in the hall of the Supreme Rada, there was utter chaos. The deputies were meeting and simply incapable of coming to a decision about what to do next. Those deputies with white bands around their heads—the hunger strikers—stood out among them. They invited the students' representative, Donii, to speak. He demanded (and got) a live broadcast that evening, all the while addressing Kravchuk as "Mister Leonid." Kravchuk, exhausted by the struggle, whether with the students or with democratic bloc or with his Communist party colleagues, which had obviously completely unnerved him, stood up through the whole thing.

That evening the leaders of the hunger strikers appeared live on television. They explained their demands at some length, criticizing parliament and the party. One boy, an Afghanistan veteran, related how, one month after his induction into the army, he was sent off to the war. Their fearful exhaustion made a strong impression—their burning eyes, their caved-in cheeks. They were all hoarse; all had caught cold. One of them spoke so feebly that it seemed he was on the point of fainting. They mentioned that some had already ended up in the resuscitation unit, among them an anarchist from Irkutsk who was observing a "dry" fast, refusing even water.

On Tuesday the tension increased even more. The students from the university seized the university's Red block, erected barricades to keep the teachers out and hoisted a blue-and-yellow flag. They called this an "occupation strike." The institutes were no longer functioning. From morning to night young demonstrators walked along Khreshchatyk. There were more and more police ardently defending the television station for fear that someone would again occupy it. It all looked as though a revolution had begun.

I ran into Vitalii Donchyk, one of the leaders of the Democratic party, on Khreshchatyk. Some man was with him, a teacher from a professional technical college, who listlessly explained that young people simply don't want to study. But his arguments rang rather hollow.

At the same time, that morning in parliament deputy Reva from the Crimea proposed the introduction of a state of emergency. Those who were listening to the live broadcast on radio were shocked out of their wits, thinking, "Well, here it is—the end."

However, the voice of reason prevailed, and after long and nerve-wracking debates they agreed to strike a co-ordinating committee comprising five men each from the "majority" and "minority" plus Ivan Pliushch from the Presidium of the Supreme Rada, who does not belong to any bloc.

While members were being appointed to the co-ordinating committee, Les Taniuk, chair of the cultural affairs commission, called Kotsiuba, chair of the legal commission, delegated by the "majority," a "political prostitute." Later he effectively apologized before the deputies and before Kotsiuba for himself, and on behalf of Lenin, who liked to refer to his political opponents in the same way. This was the parliamentary tone and style of the day.

Tension was growing in the city; someone even saw tanks in one neighborhood. Perhaps they were armored vehicles, but we all call them tanks. That evening and the following day, the co-ordinating committee sat, and parliament followed the agenda, but it was obvious they were distracted and preoccupied.

On Wednesday morning the minister of Public Health announced that the state of the students' health was critical and that he declined all responsibility for the consequences. On the same day a column of workers from "Arsenal," our biggest factory, and, what's more, an armaments maker, marched to the parliament. They shouted one word: Arsenal. And that was the last straw. At last, late Wednesday evening, the co-ordinating committee reported that negotiations with the students had concluded and that all their demands would be met. That is: no Union treaty before ratification of the constitution; no soldier from Ukraine posted outside the boundaries of Ukrainian territory except on a voluntary basis; immediate drafting of a law on the referendum and the holding of a referendum on confidence in the existing parliament; the creation of a commission on the nationalization of party property; and, finally, the resignation of Prime Minister Masol. Representatives of the students were in the hall. When Kravchuk read out the resolution, they stood up and hugged one another, while the deputies who had been on hunger strike threw off their white headbands. Most of the deputies applauded.

On the evening of the same day a rally was held in the

square. It continued until Thursday, that is, until this morning.

The strike somewhat obscured—and at the same time occasioned—the biggest literary event of the past week: the resignation from the CPSU-CPU of Oles Honchar, the very embodiment of stagnation as well as an idol of the sixties. He won the Stalin prize for his novel, *The Standard Bearers*; then, in the 1960s, he was harassed for his novel, *The Cathedral*; then Brezhnev himself, it seems, added his name in the 1970s to the list of members of the Central Committee of the CPSU. He was in the Party 47 years, for 30 years was a deputy of the Supreme Soviet of the USSR and who knows how many years a member of the Central Committee. He wavered for many months, but what finally got to him was that his granddaughter Lesia went to assist the hunger strikers in the square. Concerning his statement, the newspapers have written, and the radio broadcast, that Honchar is a well-known figure in Ukraine and that in spite of everything else he is still head of the official and officious Committee for the Defense of Peace.

At the Writers' Union, the true believers who had entreated with him are, understandably, in shock. Honchar, who during the decades of his "canonization" had become an idol in his own way, has dealt a real blow to the Writers' Union party organization, which not so long ago was led by that other "classic" of stagnation and now one of Gorbachev's court poets—Borys Oliinyk. These days as a rule we pronounce his last name in the Russian manner: Oleinik.

An interesting detail about the CP. The regional committees require references from the party organization when people quit the party. What for, do you think? Do they really hope that everything will go back to what it was and they will settle accounts with the "former members"?

In spite of all that, Kiev is having an exceptionally mild and pleasant autumn. The days are very warm, the leaves on the trees have turned a particularly vivid gold color, every day the sky is a deep blue (much like the sky of the Canadian north). On such a day all you want to do is stroll in the streets, to loll about and languish in the last heat of the season.

All the more since in our city apartments and at the office

it is unbelievably stifling, and this is one more prank of our socialist management. On a certain day, as a rule on October 1, some official turns on the heat in three million residences throughout the whole city, all the radiators in all the apartments heat up—and the buildings with them—and so when it's 15 degrees outside, inside it's 40. You walk around nude, drenched in sweat, opening all the doors and windows to let some bit of breeze in, and at the same time you read in the papers that there is an energy crisis in the country, and that it's necessary to open new atomic energy plants. So we still live according to principles of the absurd.

Owing to political passions, the wonderful weather and a rather romantic mood, I've done very little work lately; but I have written, as commissioned by the members, statutes of the Women's Society of Rukh, in a decidedly feminist key. Now I'm waiting to hear what the members have to say. I expect the reaction will be ambivalent.

P.S. October 22

A couple of days after everything had subsided, the students had dismantled their camp, and the square had been swept and washed down, a deputy from the democratic bloc related, confidentially, that on Monday Kravchuk had apparently turned to Gorbachev with the request that he introduce martial law in Kiev. And that Gorbachev apparently refused. Maybe it's the Nobel prize that saved us, or maybe just common sense. I don't know. Maybe it's all just run-of-the-mill rumors.

D[mytro] P[avlychko] told me that on Monday he experienced a terrible spiritual depression, a real crisis. "I feel as if I were about to be shot," he said. Everybody who was following the debates about the hunger strikers felt that same depression on Monday, but probably not everyone felt that he might be executed.

Of course, execution is a metaphor (I would like to think), but some metaphors float around only in the head of a

Ukrainian statesman educated by Soviet history.

I drove by taxi across the square where the strikers' tents used to be and the taxi driver, a young man, said: "It's too bad the students have gone; while they were here, there was somewhere to go, to have a talk...." Kiev after the strike and the student disturbances has become another city. It's gone through its initiation.

But I know the victory is only temporary.

October 29

Today the Second Congress of Rukh, or, more precisely, the Second All-Ukrainian Assembly of Rukh, concluded. This was an extraordinary event which attracted wide-spread attention in Kiev and, I should say, in Ukraine generally. The papers are writing about it and television news carrying commentaries with a basically positive accent. Thus, in attitude and openness, the contrast with last year's constituent assembly is striking.

For several days before the opening of Rukh's congress, welcoming banners displaying the trident were hung on Khreshchatyk and other downtown streets, something along the lines of : "From all-Ukrainian unity to a united Ukraine!" In this spot, some mindless Soviet placards always used to be hung, of the sort saying, "Peace! Labor! May!" or, "Long Live the Great October Socialist Revolution!"

The congress lasted four days, perhaps a little too long; all the same, not nearly everyone who had wanted to speak managed to do so. There was a constant percolation of discussion on this theme, the rank and file in the hall demanding a chance to speak, the presidium placating them, explaining that not all 2,000 participants could speak. (Only 10% of them, by the way, were women.)

All this took place in the finest, most important hall of the republic—the Ukraine Palace—where the party congresses always used to be held. When I was still a schoolgirl, I was in this hall for some Komsomol gathering and heard a speech by

First Secretary Volodymyr Shcherbytsky. Volodymyr Yavoriv-sky said that, if Shcherbytsky were suddenly to wake up in his grave and see all these "nationalists," "extremists," and other "destructive elements" in the beloved palace where he used to address the communists, he'd probably decide never to wake up again.

The delegates and guests formed quite an exotic crowd. Cossacks with their topknots, old men in the uniforms of the Sich Riflemen, hundreds in embroidered shirts, almost all with little blue-and-yellow flags on their lapels, or some other symbol, and among them some businessmen or guests from the West who stood out with their checked, silk ties, elegant ladies from the Union of Ukrainian Women—all this composed a rather aesthetic picture. During the breaks, the Cossacks sang, gentlemen from the diaspora filmed it all on video, and fans gathered around superstar parliamentary deputies, demanding autographs.

Interestingly, in such a crowd I didn't encounter many whom I knew. Some of those who started out a year ago have already left, and altogether unfamiliar faces predominated. This is very important: earlier, at such assemblies, you'd always meet people from the same circle—writers, intellectuals, academics. Now there are fewer of them and many more from other walks of life. On the other hand, there's something here to give one pause. If intellectuals and academics are leaving Rukh, this could be catastrophic for it. In fact, such a process is already discernible. At the same time, the main appeal, which rings out in almost every speech, is that while we have intellect on our side, we do not have real power, but it is by intelligence itself that we will emerge victorious over those who have only power.

The congress opened with greetings to Metropolitan Mstyslav, who finally has got his visa and has arrived to stay on in Kiev and lead the Ukrainian Autocephalous church.

Ivan Drach, who chaired the first day of the meeting, showed up in an embroidered shirt, obviously to demonstrate his loyalty to the people. (D[mytro] P[avlychko] did the same on the second day.) We were deluged by populism in various external and verbal forms. The point isn't even in the national costumes but in the tone of the majority of the speeches: to say those words which were the most pleasing, comprehensible and appropriate for this large and highly agitated, excited assembly.

Under the direction of Ivan Drach, the executive was quickly voted in, then Drach delivered his scheduled report. I'm not going to bother describing what Drach and the other speakers had to say—all this you can read, study and analyze even better than I. (If only because for you it's all just theory which you can apprehend coolly and aloofly, while for me it's real life.) But I'll mention a few of the chief impressions which seem to me, today, right after the congress, to be the quintessence of what was said.

In the first place, a triviality. Rukh has expunged from its name the word "perestroika." I'm awfully glad about that, because I never did like the word or the notion, imposed on us by Gorbachev and his Communist party as some kind of big myth. For that reason, Drach, as usual speaking metaphorically, said: "No matter how much you reconstruct the slaughterhouse, it's still a slaughterhouse." It has become obvious all on its own this year that nobody in Rukh wants to reconstruct and improve the Empire, but only to kiss it good-bye.

Propped up for five and a half years, "perestroika" is finished. It has no prospects and, as a concept advanced by the imperial center, has become reactionary.

So the congress confirmed the course of departure from the USSR, the building of a sovereign state—which is now the chief task on the agenda—and attempted to elaborate the strategy and tactics of this departure and this state-building.

Up to now, Rukh has been in large part spontaneous, amateur and unprofessional. It fought for the right of free speech and against slander; it mobilized new members. (In the east, of course, these tasks remain absolutely vital.) A lot was said about this, and about the mistakes of the leadership and of Rukh as a whole. As Volodymyr Cherniak said: "We've done a good job, but we have to proceed differently now."

The word "crisis" came up rather frequently, but this

crisis must be understood correctly, for Rukh has grown a lot in a year and now has close to 5 to 6 million members and supporters. In part the crisis consists in the fact that dozens of parties have been created during this last year; their members are also members of Rukh and among their leaders are individual leaders of Rukh. The danger exists that Rukh will fragment into parties and grouplets, dissipating its forces. Viacheslav Chornovil underscored it: "If Rukh becomes indistinguishable from the parties, it will disappear; it will fail."

For this reason Serhii Konev proposed the creation of a political coalition of democratic forces, "Democratic Ukraine," with a single list of candidates for the future elections, a single nominee for the presidency, for which position the bloc leader should be chosen with the aim of creating a non-communist government of national salvation. It's immediately obvious that Rukh and the CP are the main political forces. Rukh's aim is to remove communists from all spheres of power. This tendency toward anti-communism was affirmed and given a legal base by Serhii Holovaty, who is turning into an ever more dazzling orator.

Much was said about the CP and its frantic financial activity, which is meant to defend it against the possible nationalization of its property. As well, the CP, with its enterprises and banks, is organizing joint enterprises with foreign capital, and the foreigners are co-operating in rather unprincipled fashion. They debated whether a communist can be a member of Rukh and, although many (e.g., Porovsky) spoke against it, they kept on as members those rank-and-file communists who support the aims of Rukh.

This decisive transitional period which has begun in Ukraine demands intelligence and knowledge. Rukh's ideologues said that it is now time to work out a concept of the future order in Ukraine and to prepare for leadership. But here's the rub: the delineation of the concept and its embodiment in practice require professionalism and a businesslike manner, which is just what was missing in many reports. Regrettably, there were many who simply repeated that our enemies are Bolshevism and communism, the KGB and the imperial "center," but proposed no concrete ideas, and discussed amendments to the program and statutes with obvious lack of interest.

The hall waxed euphoric at every sensational criticism of the existing regime. Crying "Glory!" all stood up to applaud; the moderators begged them in turn not to indulge in standing ovations and prolonged applause, in order to save time, but no one paid attention. People are still so astonished at seeing and hearing that which they are in fact seeing and hearing—their favorite deputies (Lukianenko, Chornovil, Horyn, Altunian, Larysa Skoryk, Yavorivsky and many others), exotic foreign guests (among whom were a representative of some American congressman, a Canadian minister, members of the Polish, Bulgarian and Romanian parliaments, some foreign millionaires, representatives of all the national fronts of the republics of the USSR, and a mob of foreign and domestic journalists). Whenever any of the foreigners, in his welcoming remarks, said, "Glory to Ukraine!" (and they all said it), the hall gave him a standing ovation. (I almost never stood up, and my neighbors looked askance at me as if at an opportunist.) The moderators practically begged the audience, "Don't stand up, don't applaud so long, let's save some time," but to no avail. Perhaps I ask too much of my colleagues in Rukh, but I so much want us finally to make the transition from rallies to purposeful and calm work. Because there has long been no need for us to convince one another of anything.

And yet the romantic period has ended or is about to, without a doubt. As Yavorivsky said, "The time has come to discard the Cossack cloak and roll up our sleeves," i.e., to get down to work to transform Rukh into the predominant political force in Ukraine.

Even before the congress, various rumors and speculations were circulating in our political circles about who was going to be put up as the leader of Rukh. In fact, two candidacies seemed to be most likely—Serhii Holovaty and Mykhailo Horyn. In the end, the Great Council of Rukh, which met a week before the congress, resolved to elect Horyn, who was chairman of the Secretariat. There was a lot of talk in the corridors as well, since the leader of Rukh must give it direction, even provide its very conception. Holovaty impressed the younger people and the intellectuals; Horyn was the choice of the people from Lviv and Rivne, and the members of the Ukrainian Republican party. But the unforeseen occurred at the congress. Quite unexpectedly for many, Drach, who a few months ago had announced that he intended to step down, was once again elected. D[mytro] P[avlychko], who was co-ordinating the elections, played a decisive role in this. According to the statutes, the chairman of Rukh is elected every two years, and the congress essentially confirmed Drach's chairmanship. Very few voted against him (about 250), but in the corridors the supporters of the Ukrainian Republican party expressed their dissatisfaction that D[mytro] P[avlychko] had "made" Drach chair and that this was a choice allegedly favored by the CPSU itself.

Between the supporters and members of the Ukrainian Republican party and all the others ("former atheists and activists," as Yevhen Sverstiuk put it) a veiled verbal polemic is being waged. The former claim the moral high ground, arguing that even in the dangerous times of the past they held the very same ideas they espouse today, and insinuating that you can't believe those who so recently supported the unprincipled social system. They're talking about Drach, D[mytro] P[avlychko], Yavorivsky and all those who had been in the CPSU, including those who, like me, came too late to provide much support for the unprincipled system, but did nothing directly to overthrow it. Sverstiuk, who as you know spent many years in prison and exile, went so far as to say, "Now comes the time of the demagogues." His own report on the religious question, which called for morality in Rukh, had this point as its central thesis—the important question is not whom you are for or against, but who you *are*. Sverstiuk is an activist of the Ukrainian Autocephalous Orthodox church.

And although Rukh was further from a split than at its first congress, the possibility did not fully recede. So, in light of this often invisible struggle, and struggle by innuendo, the election of Drach signifies a certain *status quo* that must be preserved in the leadership in order to satisfy both easterners and westerners, radicals and former communists.

Fortunately, there were no such appeals as "Ukraine for the Ukrainians," although the Organization of Ukrainian Nationalists activists could hardly contain themselves and much was said about relations between the nationalities, especially between Ukrainians and Jews. It's true that today Rukh encourages the Jews and promotes their culture, but they continue to leave Ukraine in droves. There are broad economic and political reasons for this.

Yesterday, I went home in a taxi that I caught near the Ukraine Palace. The driver asked me, "Are you from Rukh?" I answered that I was. And he bluntly replied, "I don't trust any of you. Rukh is a political prostitute. At first you said you support the Communist party and now you make speeches against it." We drove for ten minutes, during which I tried to find out from him just what he does believe in, whether in the CPSU or in Lenin, who were not merely prostitutes but quite simply murderers. But he did not even want to listen to me.

There isn't much ground for euphoria. Everything still lies ahead, and not even virtual famine, which we have now in Ukraine, has fully aroused the people. And the danger of an army coup or of martial law looms over us. (The introduction of martial law in some parts of Moldova electrified the hall yesterday to the nth degree.) And, although in his talk Chornovil said that martial law would be the last gasp of the regime, its catastrophe, I'm wondering if it would not also be the last gasp in the life of very real, living people.

The congress concluded today on an unpleasant note. The Patriarch of Moscow, Aleksii the Second, arrived in Kiev, ostensibly to grant sovereignty to the Russian Orthodox church in Ukraine, now renamed the Ukrainian Orthodox church. This is the sovereignty of a daughter church, hence incomplete and ambiguous. Today he was to conduct a service in the Cathedral of St. Sophia. Rukh had sent the patriarch a telegram suggesting that the Moscow church decline the idea of conducting a service in this most important Ukrainian sanctuary. This, naturally, didn't go over. So, in the morning, pickets and commandos stood in the square, Mykhailo Horyn and Oles Shevchenko lay down on the pavement to obstruct the passage of the patriarch's automobile, and the police dragged them away by their feet. They took the patriarch around to the back door and, during the service, there were clashes on the square between believers of both confessions. Autocephalists, or perhaps provocateurs, beat up a monk from the Caves Monastery.

I'm thinking about what Ukraine will be like by the third congress of Rukh and whether it will survive in its role as a coalition of democratic forces, whether independent workers' trade unions and strike committees will support it, whether it will fade into the shadows as new political forces appear on the scene from student or worker movements. And I cannot give any definitive answer.

And I think about whether I will be a participant in the third congress or whether I'll go back to my studies, following the example of those colleagues who have already done so. And I can't answer that definitively either.

Everything still operates in the old way, in the sense of the unpredictability of each successive day, whether in political or personal life.

As for the sincere envy of our "very interesting" life—when "history is being made"—among numerous Ukrainians in the diaspora (they repeat this endlessly), this "interesting life" can be psychologically very difficult, even insupportable, because of its very unpredictability, and because the "better future" is cloaked in a thick fog of obscurity.

November 7

Today is the "great" communist holiday, October Revolution Day. The 73rd anniversary. I'm one of those who consider this a day of mourning. But at this moment, the festival's military parade, the communists' demonstration, and the funereal rally of the anticommunists are all behind us. The sun is shining and everyone seems all right, even though my mood is not the best. But let's take things in order. There have been a great many events this past week that have shaken people, even stirred them up, and others which have touched only our family.

The end of last month, October 30, was marked in Kiev by a new panic. On Monday, rumors circulated that, as of November 1, according to a decision of the Council of Ministers, coupons for all goods more expensive than 20 kopecks would be introduced throughout Ukraine. A coupon is a piece of paper divided into squares; on each square a certain sum is indicated—one ruble, three, five, ten, even one hundred. You go to the store, pay for the goods with money, then the shopkeeper takes a pair of scissors and clips the coupon. This is called the "consumer card." What is this supposed to accomplish? The idea is that only those who earn wages receive coupons, and that the coupons are based on 70% of their earnings. Anyone who doesn't have a steady income in Ukraine—e.g., visitors who buy everything up or locals, who likewise buy everything up wholesale and sell it on the black market—will be left out, hungry and naked. The problem is that millions of people don't have steady incomes or have only minimal earnings. All of us—formerly rather privileged and comfortable thanks to literary honoraria—now find ourselves partly among the poor. Thus, I've been given coupons according to my miserable academic salary, that is, 100 rubles' worth of coupons per month. But I receive no coupons for my honoraria—and for one article I am often paid four times my monthly salary. Of course, I can survive as before, shopping only in the private sector, i.e., the market. But in one day, as of November 1, the prices there have risen astronomically. A kilo of meat costs 20 rubles, and everything else has gone up proportionately. Soon all this will be beyond my means.

My parents' situation is almost comical. Mother doesn't work, so she gets no salary from the state; my sister gets a small student stipend, so her coupons are worth only 50 rubles. D[mytro] P[avlychko], who gets a huge state salary, is the only one of us permitted to hold coupons, but hasn't received any.

They told him at the Supreme Rada that they still haven't been issued coupons for deputies. So he went to Moscow (for talks with Shevardnadze) and then immediately to Lviv with mother, taking my miserable 100 rubles' worth of coupons.

All these coupons—which were instantly referred to as "Masolyky" (their introduction was Masol's last decree)—have still another dimension, the psychological. On November 1, pay day, *everyone* showed up at work at our institute. They all wanted to have a look at the coupons. Everyone was feeling depressed, even crushed, by this turn of events. My own spirits were so low that I carried this faded blue piece of paper, which even bore my surname and place of work, as though it were a toad in my hand. In all sincerity, I found it offensive and incredibly insulting to our unhappy people to have survived thus far only to be reduced to such a fate.

Later that same day I ran into a group of my poet-friends, with Rymaruk heading them up, near the Writers' Union. They're almost all unemployed literati who have no steady work, and therefore no coupons. We stopped at the Aeneas Bar for a cognac. We stood around, each taking a turn at cursing the Soviet authorities, then we left. I should add that this was all carried off in a conventional literary form—street curses. These days spitefulness is the dominant mood in the streets.

Right up to the last day, parliament knew nothing about the action of the Council of Ministers, and on the 30th something close to panic was unleashed in the Supreme Rada. The democrats, caught by surprise by the government's secretly planned action, protested, rather dispiritedly. Kravchuk's deputy, Hryniov, spoke particularly harshly against this system of coupons. Fokin from the government and the minister of trade tried to explain that they themselves didn't understand and asserted that these coupons were devised to protect the Ukrainian market. That this is a step toward a Ukrainian currency. The opposition has long insisted on the necessity of introducing a Ukrainian currency, but the "right" is dead set against it, realizing that Ukrainian hard currency could be the first concrete step away from the Union. As a result, the Supreme Rada approved the government's measures, as usual ambiguous and ill-considered.

Speculation in coupons began immediately. And tension in the city, which had abated somewhat after the triumph of the students, once again peaked. It is all reminiscent of that "Polish variation" with which the economists frightened all of us five years ago and which, in the end, it seems we have not been able to avoid. On November 2, the first spontaneous riots against the coupons took place on Kirov Street, with private cars blocking off the street near the Supreme Rada. We watched all this from the windows of the institute. A savage mood is growing among the people in connection with these coupons. Statements such as, "I'd take a machine gun and shoot the commies and wouldn't give a damn for the consequences," are quite common.

The Supreme Rada still hasn't elected anyone to the post of prime minister. Kravchuk has put forward five candidates one after another. Some, having put forward their programs, prudently withdrew. Then the "right" turned down Pylypchuk, author of the program of Ukraine's transition to the market, and the democratic bloc boycotted the elections when, after the rejection of the democrat Pylypchuk, Kravchuk nominated a partocrat. But everyone's used to constant crisis in parliament and ordinary people long ago stopped following its sessions.

Another thing weighing down the atmosphere of the city since the beginning of November was the approach of the October festivities. Following tradition, a military parade was planned for Khreshchatyk in Kiev, because it is the capital of a military district. A similar parade was planned for Moscow, but deputies from Moscow council and ordinary activists laid themselves down in front of the tanks right at the rehearsals. In Kiev they had also always conducted such rehearsals, but now they were afraid to do so. The democratic bloc in the city council tried to introduce a motion banning the parade, but didn't have a majority. The partocrats walked out, breaking the quorum.

The opposition addressed the presidium of the Supreme Rada with an analogous request, but were refused. Then the opposition issued a declaration which Mykhailo Horyn read out. "The revolution, carried out in a foreign state, brought our people hunger, suffering, destruction...." In response to this declaration, the partocrats had one of their own about the October Revolution as the most momentous event of the twentieth century, and how socialist values are humanist values, and other such ravings. Then Mosiuk, deputy mayor of Kiev, took the floor with an appeal to the Supreme Rada to cancel the parade, considering the tense situation in the city, but at this the partocrat deputies ostentatiously left the hall. I don't know whether in other countries the majority sometimes walks out of meetings... Parliament recessed until November 12, having given sanction to that repulsive parade of soldiers and tanks in downtown Kiev. However, on November 5, the city council had already decided to lead a parade not in the city center but on Victory Square, where they had already built a platform for the government. For their demonstration, the Communists got Khreshchatyk with its two Lenin monuments, while Rukh and other democrats got Bohdan Khmelnytsky Square.

On the evening of November 6, a group of students and activists occupied a section of Victory Square to block the soldiers' passage, but at night they were brutally knocked about and dispersed by the commandos.

So, on the morning of November 7, a rather brief and somewhat uncertain military parade took place. At the obelisk, without a platform (!) stood Kravchuk, Pliushch and Hurenko and members of the government, although clearly not all of them. Hryniov, Kravchuk's deputy, wasn't there. General Gromov, our dwarfish Afghan avenger with the metallic voice and the metallic blue eyes, made a speech in Russian. "We will pronounce a decisive 'No!' to all extremists, nationalists, separatists... We will not yield, we will not allow...we will defend the gains of the revolution...the greatest event of the twentieth century." And so on, in the same vein. It seemed that even Kravchuk and the government listened to this tirade with rather sour expressions. Then the army marched past, in the rain, then the armored vehicles and rockets. And that was it. The military vehicles drove up the boulevard with the intention of proceeding along Khreshchatyk, but parliamentary deputies, with Mykhailo Horyn in the lead, were blocking the road near St. Vladimir's Cathedral.

(In Moscow, all this was more pretentious and vulgar. Gorbachev stood atop the Lenin mausoleum and made a pro-communist speech; the latest model tanks and rockets drove across Red Square.... The cold wind of a turn to the right has been blowing this last while from Moscow. Gorbachev's decrees and edicts are becoming ever more conservative. Even his position on the Persian Gulf raises doubts; i.e., the rigidity of anti-Iraqi directives. They're even talking about the possibility of Shevardnadze's resignation.)

After the military parade, the Ukrainian government scurried over to the other end of Shevchenko Boulevard, and on the steps near the Lenin monument joined the communist rally. All the approaches to Victory Square and to Khreshchatyk were blocked by huge trucks so you couldn't drive across, and by police so you couldn't walk across. Only those with invitations could enter. (It was obvious who had them.) All the same, this rally was rather listless. The crowd stood expressionless, as though frozen. An old veteran yelled out enthusiastically that we've come along and will go on further still toward the bright future (he spoke in Russian). A few female voices dispiritedly called out, "Hurrah." Probably as a joke. Then they all walked over to the next Lenin monument, led by Kravchuk and Hurenko.

At the same time, all those to whom Gromov had urged us to declare a decisive "Nyet!" were gathering on Bohdan Khmelnytsky Square. There weren't an awful lot of people here either. It was difficult to say anything new about the revolution from this point of view. Rather, there was an event—the communist demonstration—that necessitated a response. In the morning, before the rally, there had been a clash between those carrying red Soviet flags and those carrying blue-and-yellow ones.

It was very cold and the anti-October rally concluded quickly, moving over to the Shevchenko monument. The police, in evidence as never before, had gradually begun to disperse. I went to my sister's to support her in a rather unpleasant situation in which our family had found itself.

It happened like this. On Sunday, November 4 at 6:00 p.m., someone poured red paint over the door of my parents' apartment and on the floor and walls of the building entrance. (I happened to be at their place at the time, D[mytro] P[avlychko] and mother having gone to Lviv.) It was a very sobering sight. The paint on the door and on the white walls was meant to symbolize blood, and blood is what it looked like. For five hours, Lana washed the door down with alcohol, which diluted the paint, and I anxiously pondered the significance of the incident. In the meantime, someone called several times on the telephone and hung up. We didn't call the police, speculating that it was the work of hoodlums and not wanting to upset our parents.

The next morning, a man rang up, representing himself as a member of the Organization of Ukrainian Nationalists and saying that D[mytro] P[avlychko] was hindering them in their work and that they would make another Halan out of him (Halan was assassinated). Thoroughly frightened, my sister called me up and I, completely bewildered, called Drach, but he wasn't at home; so then I rang Pavlo Movchan. He informed the higher police authorities at once, detectives arrived, conducted an investigation and even left behind a machine that registers the phone number of everyone who phones D[mytro] P[avlychko]'s apartment. No one called again, or called and hung up. After thinking about it long and hard, Lana phoned our parents in Lviv. Of course this spoiled their mood.

It's terrible to think that the threat might be serious. You want to believe that this is psychological terror, because it's too terrible to think about planned provocation; but what's even more terrifying is to think of an unknown schizophrenic who, for some reason, is looking for revenge. But such is the character of our life that we're not very accustomed to count on common sense or elementary logic. What would the murder of one oppositionist, even a prominent one, achieve? Nothing. You can't stop what's unfolding. Yet they murdered Men, the Russian priest and human rights activist, not so long ago. And have never found the killers.

Before my eyes is the bloody paint on the door of my parents' apartment.

But let's go back a bit, this time to my own experiences. That is, to my painful theme, my version of an *idée fixe*. On November 2, at our institute, there was supposed to be a party meeting following upon the one in May when the first six members quit the CPSU. Over the summer another 20 declared their intention to quit. They included all the most intelligent and talented scholars in our institute, leaving behind the pensioners and the "meritorious old-timers," such as Leonid Mykhailovych Novychenko, who, after the war, worked in the ideological branch of the Central Committee of the CPU, or Stepan Andriiovych Kryzhanivsky, one of the authors of the legendary collective poem, "Ode to the Great Stalin from the Ukrainian People," or Dmytro Volodymyrovych Zatonsky, son of a CPU activist repressed in the 1930s. This is our living history; they built if not a system then the canons of socialism. Besides them, among the communists at the institute, are various idlers and cynics who lived very well in the past and live rather well even now, former "writers of denunciations," whose names everyone knows and who themselves know that we know (a piquant psychological situation). There are also various pseudo-scholars who spent decades writing their dissertations and never did finish them but stuck to the institute, bound by some kind of enigmatic, non-academic ties. There are some phlegmatic but very decent people incapable of any decisive actions. Life somehow carried them into the CPSU and to leave, to take action, is difficult for them. And then there is, naturally, our valiant, three-man directorship which of course does not believe in the irreversible approach of what we call political pluralism. Altogether there are about 60 such people.

You should have seen how they gathered in the hall for the party meeting. You should have seen our darkened corridor at six o'clock in the evening and how they stood around and circled near the hall, lowering their heads when one of the "formers" walked past them; for our part, we—former communists, current extremists and even members of other parties—quite consciously and defiantly loitered in the vicinity. In the end, the communists did not make up a quorum and the meeting didn't take place. Partly because their current boss was hurrying to some drinking spree and didn't press anyone into the hall. So they stood around, turning away their heads and lowering their eyes, as though they were ashamed of something.

Our Georgian, Sandro Mushkudiani, beaming all over with satisfaction and almost taking flight off the floor in spite of his corpulence, consoled and cheered up the "extremists" that day. The democrats had won the elections in Georgia. Undoubtedly, Georgia will separate from the Union and its president will be our colleague, the literary expert and dissident, a true prince and son of a classic Georgian writer, Zviad Gamsakhurdia.[43] And we joke that our colleague Mushkudiani will be Georgia's ambassador to Ukraine.

A rather interesting theater season is beginning on this eve of the "October holidays' in Kiev. Our theater now operates without censorship or aesthetic restrictions imposed by functionaries from the Ministry of Culture. Thus unfettered, it has become avant-garde and experimental (staging experiments that theater in the West went through twenty years ago, of course). Except for ultra-aesthetes and theater hounds, though, almost no one goes to theater these days.

I've recently seen two very good performances. The premiere, at the Youth Theater, on the day they introduced the coupons, of that old, well-known play of Peter Weiss, *Marat/Sade*, was very timely. The French National Assembly at the time of the revolution, with madmen and madwomen playing the deputies, reminded us of the Ukrainian parliament, although the director added not a single word of his own to the text. And the style of performance was emphatically theatrical, subtle in its absurdism—the domicile of the mad where the drama of the revolution was played out.

The other play, *O-O-I* (Chernobyl)—a new production by the young director/experimentalist, Andrii Zholdak—is a symbolic conceptualization of the apocalypse of our lives. This drama of symbols where nothing is said directly, where everything is oblique, nevertheless has a clear theme: apocalypse, debilitation, degeneration of our system. The language is patois and obscenity and street rap. The performance takes place in the hallway of one of Kiev's institutes and the set is a garbage dump and pitful of slops. You could call its atmosphere black humor.

The key scene: some ragged proles savagely murder a blind man, then one of the murderers goes blind and calls out at the same time that he sees the light of the future. And they all go forward with hysterical cries to this luminous future. Imagine it: the next morning (I saw the play on November 6) that veteran on the square near Lenin shouted the same thing with same kind of hysteria: "And we will go on building the bright future!"

But which is more theatrical, theater or real life?

And how's life over there? What's new with you and the CIUS? I remember my tranquil university life in Edmonton, where I missed the political passions of Kiev; now, at home, I miss the quiet university life all the more.

November 15

The events of the last days show that the right wing has gone on the offensive. The party newspapers have finally got their nerve back and, in their reports about the Rukh congress, mention that there were only portraits of Bandera and nationalists in Ukrainian Insurgent Army uniforms to be seen there, and appeals to terror. A brutal anti-Rukh statement from the Politburo of the Central Committee of the Communist Party of Ukraine was published today. In its top stories of the day, the Moscow television program *Vremia* showed, along with the crisis in the Persian Gulf, how the workers at the shipyards in Mykolaiv assembled at a rally (probably at lunch break, for they stood around looking rather sullen) and demanded the immediate signing of the Union accord. (This Mykolaiv factory produces warships, among other things, and its workers work for the military. A disarmed and independent Ukraine would be inconvenient for them.)

A crowd with red Soviet flags has shown up in place of the crowds with blue-and-yellow flags at the parliament building. These are the delegates, in from Odessa and other southern Ukrainian oblasts, who are demanding adherence to "socialist choice" and a single, united Soviet army. They are protesting the "bourgeois-nationalist" choice that the opposition wants to impose on Ukraine. They are never dispersed, even though that inauspicious law prohibiting all demonstrations at a distance of less than 1,000 meters from the Supreme Rada is still on the books. So, the "Reds" stand around and shout, "Down with Pavlychko!" (D[mytro] P[avlychko] noticed a secretary of one of the Kiev-area party regional committees in the crowd), "Down with Drach!", "Down with Chornovil!" and, most frequently, "Down with Khmara!"

But who's going to disperse them when even the police themselves organized pickets near the Supreme Rada on November 12, the day when parliament resumed working after a brief recess? The police demanded a law on the police and the disciplining of deputies Mykhailo Horyn and Serhii Holovaty, who had taken part in the "disturbances" on St. Sophia's Square on October 28. And especially the disciplining of the deputy Stepan Khmara, but more about that later.

(At the same time, Khreshchatyk was being blocked by private taxi drivers with their own demand: the abrogation of the sale of gasoline by coupon. However, gasoline has not been available, nor is there any now, with or without coupons.)

We now call our system "couponism." We marched forward to communism and have arrived at couponism. Thus the pun of one of the deputies.

One more detail from the eventful day of November 12—a session of the oblast council of the Crimea discussed the question of Crimean autonomy: within Ukraine, Russia or the Union. This latter variant seemed most congenial to them. Yet another plot of the partocrats who don't want to give up the Crimea, with its wonderful climate and its dozens or even hundreds of party sanatoria and dachas. What also had them exercised was how not to readmit all the Tatars exiled by Stalin, who are now laying claim to the Crimea as their historic homeland. Kravchuk showed up and promised the Crimea autonomy.

As to the particular place of Khmara in the protests near the Supreme Rada in Kiev, this can be explained by an extremely suspicious episode, bordering on provocation.

Stepan Khmara is one of the most colorful figures in parliament, a dentist from Chervonohrad (a mining town in western Ukraine, where they were the first in Ukraine to pull down a Lenin monument), an ex-prisoner of the Gulag who served seven years (1980-87), and member of the radical faction in the opposition. A person who, conceding no compromise with the regime, is in a position to accuse everyone, even his colleagues in the opposition, of collaboration. He is ardent, fierce, maniacal, impetuous, neurotic, uncompromising (it is quite possible that prison undermined his nervous system) and, besides that, someone who is easily provoked. Moreover, this is a system which hates him personally—this man over-flowing with a violent hatred toward it—and wants to rid itself of him at any cost. Thus, what happened with Khmara, in my opinion, could have happened only to him and not to anyone else.

It's paradoxical but a fact nevertheless that, along with other deputies, he signed an appeal on November 6 addressed to the most radical political groups and forces, foremost among them the students, not to block the military parade and the pro-communist demonstration. On November 7, together with many other deputies, he circulated in the center of town, in the districts where clashes and incidents were most likely to take place. Because, as was apparent, the most radical were by no means inclined to pay any attention to such appeals.

In the morning, before the pro-communist demonstration on Khreshchatyk, a woman approached Stepan Khmara in the underground passage and complained to him about a man who had assaulted her. This was enough to set Khmara off. Khmara went up to the man, who proceeded to shout obsceni-ties at him. At Khmara's direction, a crowd pounced on this man and found on his person a pistol and the documents of a lieutenant-colonel of the police. (It turned out that he was a colonel.) They tore at his clothes, extracting his weapon and his registration papers while he, all the while, simply went on shouting, "People, help me!" He shouted loudly enough for a video camera to record it, but not distinctly enough for passers-by or the police (who were swarming around not far off) to come effectively to his assistance. Besides, he had, up to that point, still not admitted he was a guardian of the law.

A whole detachment of police stood nearby and serenely watched from the sidelines. Then Khmara's assailants gave the pistol to the deputy Yemets, the head of the parliamentary commission on human rights, who was in the vicinity. The whole thing was filmed by two cameras, no less, and shown on t.v. on November 12.

On November 12, parliament spent almost a whole day hearing the statements of the participants in and witnesses to the Khmara incident. The "right" blatantly tried to strip deputy Khmara of his parliamentary immunity, and, as a bonus, to discredit Yemets, a deputy who enjoys tremendous popularity in Kiev.

This whole story helped the majority to push through, on the same day, a provisional resolution on the mandate commission—totally conservative in its make-up—which will take up the question of deputies' ethics.

On November 14, the procurator of Ukraine addressed an appeal to the Supreme Rada to authorize the arrest of deputy Khmara, who was accused of assaulting police colonel Hryhoriev. This was a shock of its own. Members of the opposition timorously protested but, in response to their protest, the partocrats read out telegrams signed by hundreds of policemen, workers, and collective farmers, requesting that the extremist, Khmara, and others of his ilk be disciplined. Even Roman Lubkivsky, a quiet pacifist and democrat, our Pierre Bezukhov, who has probably not once in his life raised his voice, let alone called for terror or extreme actions, found himself on the list of extremists. But at the conclusion of this debate, in which the glee and spite of the majority had been palpable, and which had poured out over the television screens, poisoning everything around, a majority—240 people—declared themselves in favor of stripping Khmara of his parliamentary immunity, which paved the way for his arrest.

When Yukhnovsky, in his usual calm and quiet voice, appealed to parliament in the name of the opposition to investigate the incident first in the mandate commission, nobody listened to him; practically hissing at him, they hooted him down.

This morning, journalists and television reporters were not admitted into the meeting hall. But the session did not last long and was adjourned until November 20.

Then the opposition held a press conference and today fifteen deputies announced their decision to hold a one-day warning hunger strike to protest the charges against Khmara.

In connection with this brouhaha, I translated, into English, a letter written by Larysa Skoryk in defence of Khmara and addressed to the women members of the European Parliament.

I was translating it and thinking that such things as the provocation against Khmara, the arrests of Rukh activists in Ternopil and Dnipropetrovsk, the paint smeared on D[mytro] P[avlychko]'s door and the threats against him on the eve of the October "holiday" could all be connected. This is, for all of us, an unambiguous cue: "Keep quiet—or we'll show you who's boss around here!"

November 17

At the Rukh meeting in our institute yesterday we drafted a telegram to protest the accusations against Khmara. It was a short, daytime meeting. In the evening, our communists attempted for the nth time to hold their own meeting and this time succeeded. But Khmara didn't interest them. They listened to another twenty-three statements of resignation of our co-workers from the party and fiery speeches from those remaining about the prospects for the communist idea, and finally tried to elect a party bureau. They didn't manage to elect a secretary—no one would agree to run. This kind of situation prevails just about everywhere. Party organizations exist, but no one's very keen on leading them.

Yesterday the parliamentary majority addressed the public with phoney calls for peace.

In Moscow, yesterday, radical deputies forced President Gorbachev to present a report about the situation in the USSR (you won't catch me writing "in our country") to the Supreme Soviet of the USSR. He has been given extraordinary powers, but his decrees disillusion both the experts and the population profoundly. What happened in Moscow at that meeting—which is continuing today—is the dramatic polarization of political forces: Gorbachev's obvious rightward drift and the growing militant opposition to him. It seems that Gorbachev seems finally to be losing touch with reality, keeps threatening the separatists, and will not entertain the possibility of the break-up of the Union. (For example, in his speech today he said that, according to his information, 70% of Ukrainians support the Union. The cameras showed the astonished faces of Fokin and Ivashko and Shcherbak's downcast look. A statement of that sort is close to being sheer demagogy.)

Moreover, the President repeated that the break-up of the state was impossible and put us all in fear of bloodshed; that is, he insisted that such a break-up could only be bloody. This had the tone of an unequivocal threat.

Yeltsin, who's supposed to be visiting Kiev on Sunday, announced that Russia is not about to repudiate its sovereignty. And then went on to propose anti-crisis measures for the whole Union. The new Ukrainian prime minister, Fokin, who was elected on the third ballot, was diplomatic. We're for sovereignty and for the Union. Which is to say, a win-win situation. The Georgians have declared that they have no intention of signing any Union treaty whatever. And so on.

What we're experiencing now is what Yeltsin calls the "paralysis of power." The all-powerful "center" is in the throes of agony. Its laws don't function. The army has been hinting that in this situation it will defend itself. From whom?

Meanwhile, D[mytro] P[avlychko] and Drach and Bohdan Horyn went off yesterday to Paris, where there is to be a conference on Monday of the Conference on Security and Co-operation in Europe. Earlier, D[mytro] P[avlychko] had travelled to see Shevardnadze to inform him that Ukraine wished to be present in the ranks of observers at this meeting. The USSR foreign minister denied this request, claiming that, no matter how favorably disposed he was, such a decision was beyond his powers. Neither Ukraine nor the Baltic republics nor Armenia was represented in the official Soviet delegation. (And this is a rather large chunk of Europe.) Nevertheless, Kravchuk signed a statement addressed to all the participating heads of state at the conference about Ukraine's intention to exercise its sovereignty in international affairs.

So the three "emissaries" have set off. There won't be much in the way of results from this, but all the same....

November 22

On Saturday the police arrested Stepan Khmara[44] right inside the Supreme Rada building. They drove him off to Lukianiv Prison, where he now sits. The same place where dozens of dissidents passed through not so long ago. More-over, Khmara's previous criminal record has not been rescinded, nor has he been rehabilitated.

There are rallies in support of Khmara in Kiev and leaflets posted all over town. They've created Khmara defence commit-tees in Galicia. The Moscow newspaper *Kommersant* observes that all this is only increasing Khmara's popularity. The procurator of Ukraine is threatening a seven-year prison term!

On Tuesday, the opposition read out its own statement of protest in parliament. The majority calculated that the Narodna Rada might just walk out of parliament. After hearing the statement, Kravchuk asked several times, in a totally confused way, as though not understanding what it was about, "Would you state clearly whether you're staying in the House or not?" It seems that a "No" wouldn't have surprised him in the least, and that in fact he might have been wishing for it. But the Narodna Rada is still in parliament, although every effort is being made to discredit it and force it out. In the circumstances, its departure would play directly into the hands of the right.

Boris Yeltsin arrived on Sunday and was very warmly received everywhere. They say that Yeltsin was afraid he'd get the same reception as Patriarch Aleksii, but he was welcomed with enthusiasm and shouts of "Hurrah!" Immediately followed by cries of "Down with Kravchuk!"

I happened to find myself near such a crowd on Monday on my way home from work. The police cordon prevented me from crossing by the trade-union building to the "Poetry" Bookstore. One Ukrainian policeman said contemptuously, "They're a bunch of pigeons." (In our slang, "pigeon" is the same as your "faggot.") This irritated me and I said that he, being a policeman, probably knew what a "pigeon" is. He replied that he knew and confirmed that that's indeed what they were. In our perverse society, it's the done thing to despise gays; not so long ago they were even imprisoned. I tried to explain to the group of young policemen how it's indecent and offensive to treat anyone with such contempt, whether "pigeons" or the "blue-and-yellows," i.e., people with flags. "Think about it. You and I are the same as these people on the square whom you've surrounded. We're alike, we have the same interests...." It's very difficult, even unbearable, to look at a face undistinguished by any kind of understanding or even a wish to understand and to try to prove something to people who don't even hear you. My experience in this regard is limited, but discouraging.

On Monday Kravchuk and Yeltsin signed a co-operation agreement between Ukraine and Russia. In all his interviews, Yeltsin repeated that this was a completely new agreement between two sovereign states. This is probably the most important element of the accord—the confirmation of each other's sovereignty. Our television network prudently refrained from showing his speech before parliament, probably because it was too trenchant for Ukraine. Meantime, at the Paris meeting of European heads of state, Gorbachev said that the chief threat to European security may now be coming from separatists and nationalists within the borders of the USSR. For a moment there, he reminded me in his speech of the late Brezhnev. Something similar in the tone of voice or in his intonation. You can see, chalked up in a crooked hand on fences around Kiev, the graffito, "Down with Gorbachev."

Chornovil has referred to the present situation in Ukraine as a "surreptitious military coup." Since Khmara's arrest the "right-wing" majority has been exploiting its numerical predominance to adopt conservative, utterly outlandish laws. For example, they approved an amendment to the provisional rules of order of the Supreme Rada to the effect that the participation of two-thirds of the deputies suffices for the validity of a parliamentary session, and that in extraordinary circumstances (such as a natural disaster or the refusal of some deputies to take part in a session) less than two-thirds represent a quorum. Thus, the majority has in fact got the better of the opposition, depriving it of all rights except those of making speeches and declarations.

Demonstrations with red Soviet flags continue to take place outside the Supreme Rada. Now the demonstrators are self-styled miners from Donetsk in snow-white miners' hard hats they're wearing for the first time, and collective farm workers from the Chernihiv region. Once more they are demanding: the immediate signing of the Union treaty, the text and terms of which they do not know, because they still haven't been published; and "the restoration of order, at last." If the first seems rather unrealistic, the second appears all too real and sinister, in light of Khmara's arrest.

Yesterday's *Radianska Ukraina* (the Communist party newspaper) came out under the slogan, "Faithful to the Red Banner."

The press and television enthusiastically publicize these demonstrations, which no one ever bothers to disperse. In the crowd are men of a certain type, whose average age is at least forty, in hats and caps, gray coats (the collective farm elite and regional party activists). Kravchuk went up to them yesterday, evidently promising "to restore order." Today the demonstrators broke up, leaving their flags behind stacked under the trees in the park and posting some guards over them. It's said they went shopping.

This turn of events has once again left me feeling very disagreeable. I catch myself thinking that my soul is on the point of utter collapse. I remember how, in the days of Brezhnev, in the news reports about official Ukrainian congresses, when all the speakers gave their talks in Russian, I would jump up and turn off the t.v. I had the unbearable feeling that this system was strangling us, destroying and crushing us; that everything Ukrainian was doomed; that soon nothing would be left of it. We didn't want to know, to think, to see, out of a normal instinct of self-preservation in order not to go mad. What galling, unrelieved powerlessness!

Something akin to this half-remembered feeling came back to me when one day the president in Moscow says we are to expect blood-letting and the next day in Kiev some activist, the obligatory proletarian or collective farm worker (he who has the last word among us) says, in Russian, "I don't understand what's going on—when is parliament going to get down to business? It's about time to restore law and order."

Another subject that throws me into the same state of stark terror is Chernobyl. For a long time now, I've simply been switching channels at the first mention of it on the television, and I read almost nothing of the newspaper articles on the subject. Why? Because psychically I cannot bear to watch children who are breathing radiation, and the elderly evacuees who return to their villages in the zone where it is dangerous to live; or to know that on much of the contaminated land even now they are planting and seeding. To survive even here in Kiev, 130 kilometers from the sarcophagus, none of this bears thinking about. Once you start thinking, there's no more sense in living. At any rate, not in making any plans for the future. The worst thing is that Chernobyl didn't teach us anything and the system which engendered it is still alive and people who defended it are still defending it. It terrifies me to think about what kind of world I live in.

Our "emissaries" have returned from Paris utterly exhausted and worn out. In the end, they were not admitted to the "summit meeting." But that wasn't as unpleasant as what happened to the Balts, who at first had been invited as observers by the French and then had the invitation canceled on the last day. But D[mytro] P[avlychko] is not disappointed in the mission, reports of which were carried in the French papers, and believes that something will come of it.

I also ran into Drach and put to him the ritual question that torments me: "Do you believe that anything will come of all your efforts?" He answered, "I have to."

November 26

Stepan Khmara has been in jail eight days already. They say he's declared a "dry" hunger strike. Seven people have been arrested in connection with this affair, among them the head of the Kiev workers' strike committee, Ratushny—the same chap who presented the demands of that futile and bootless strike on October 1 in parliament. The opposition, it seems, still hasn't recovered from its shock at Khmara's arrest. As a sign of protest, five of its members (Chornovil, Kolinets, and Boiko, inter alia) walked out of the Supreme Rada—not permanently, only temporarily—while the partocrats applauded their exit. An hysteria of the "right" swirls around this story of Khmara. The film and audio of the "beating up" of Col. Hryhoriev was shown a couple of days ago on all-Union television at the most opportune time—right after *Vremia*.

Yesterday, on Sunday, the papers published the draft of the Union treaty which is supposed to be adopted by the Congress of People's Deputies of the USSR in December.

So, this is to be a Union of so-called sovereign republics, which give up very considerable powers to the "center," i.e., to the Union. The prerogatives of the center include: adoption of the constitution, defense of sovereignty—that is, territorial integrity, declaration of war (!), organization of the army and of state security, elaboration of foreign policy, external economic activity, the organization of a single financial, credit and monetary policy and system, a single currency, a single budget, a single energy grid, transportation, roadways, a space program.... Further, as in a bad joke, republican laws take precedence in everything that does not belong to the Union's jurisdiction. In a word, nothing at all remains of the sovereignty of the republics and their declarations, unless it be the coats of arms and anthems. The Russian language is deemed to be the state language: so much for our law making Ukrainian the official language.

The text, though brief, is rather ominous. A year ago, we might have been able to accept it, but now? Dubious question. I won't go further in my analysis. Personally, I wouldn't accept a treaty even ten times more moderate that provided for any kind of center. A "commonwealth" is something else again, but this variant provokes only exasperation.

Among some opposition deputies, though, the text caused yet another shock. Everyone knew it was going to happen, but now it is confirmed. How is the opposition going to react, when it is deprived of the right to block decisions of parliament? What's going to be the reaction of the students who, a month ago, ceased their hunger strike after parliament promised not to accept a Union treaty in any form before the adoption of a constitution for Ukraine? What will be the reaction of the Organization of Soldiers' Mothers, who are insistently demanding the creation of a national army?

What new shocks await us?

Some of my learned friends in the West say, "This is impossible; it's too absurd." I would like to think so, although this is no argument for the system, which is constructed according to the laws of the absurd.

Some days ago, a strange incident occurred in Kiev that the papers have not reported at all. Near one of the Lenin monuments, the police picked up two young people—a man and a woman—stripped naked. It was rather chilly, already the end of autumn, and a small crowd had gathered when the police arrived and took these "disturbers of the peace" away. No one seems to know what this action means. Why next to

Lenin? We can only speculate.

November 29

Stepan Khmara has declared a hunger strike in prison—a dry one at that, which means he is not even drinking water and doesn't let doctors near him. They say he has a bad heart. Altunian spoke in the Supreme Rada today, requesting a review of the decision to strip Khmara of parliamentary immunity. Not bloody likely! This was before the recess. Under the pressure of the aging, gray-haired Altunian, who, all stirred up, implored the session to show mercy to his former prison-camp mate who was in danger of dying from this strike, Kravchuk put the question of whether to extend the session in order to review the case and put it to a vote. The majority voted against.

The majority is going even further on the offensive. A couple of days ago, the head of the General Staff of the Soviet army, General Moiseev, spoke to the Supreme Rada. He read a text in which he referred to Taras Shevchenko as "Comrade Shevchenko," and in which, for some reason, he referred to the Red Army throughout as the "Russian" army. Even the communist "Group of 239" smarted at this speech. The general said that he would not hear of the military service of Ukrainian citizens exclusively on Ukrainian territory, because it was tantamount to dismembering the army, 17 per cent of which is made up of recruits from Ukraine; and he made a threat to hold up the discharge of those who have already completed their term of duty from the army until the autumn call-up has been completed. That same day, the USSR minister of defence, Yazov, spoke on central television. He reminded me of the generals of Saltykov-Shchedrin: stout, with a weird hair-do, a little clump of hair (or, rather, its vestiges) combed forward over his bald spot; his too-large shoulder boards with their disproportionately large stars. A fearsome gaze, concentrated on a single point. A harsh, commanding voice which announced that, in the case of assaults upon it, the army will defend itself.

At the same time, in Zaporizhzhia, dramatic events are taking place of which the whole Soviet Union is aware. An entire air-defence regiment has refused to carry out the order to transfer its base to Semipalatinsk, in the Kazakhstan test area where nuclear tests are conducted. The wives of the officers are on hunger strike in the town's central square and the officers themselves have requested political asylum in Ukraine from Kravchuk.

One other interesting bit of news: in the Donetsk-area town of Antratsyt [Anthracite] (as the newspaper *Izvestiia* has reported), they are investigating with whose blessings and at whose expense the miners were picketing the Supreme Rada in Kiev with their red flags a couple of weeks ago. It's been revealed that they were selected and organized by the regional party committee. They were allotted a bus and a considerable stock of scarce foodstuffs, including instant coffee.

Passions are seething in Ukraine around the ill-fated coupons. Everybody now has them, but you still can't buy anything with them. There weren't any goods or products in the past and there aren't any now. My first wave of fear vis-à-vis the coupons has subsided—we have a whole pile of them at home. At the market where I do all my shopping they aren't required, but prices there have doubled again.

So, while ordinary folk run about from store to store in hope of being able to use their coupons, the politicians and the politicos are cudgeling their brains over the prospects of a Union treaty. In Moscow, an extraordinary congress of people's deputies of Russia is in its third day. Under pressure of the communists and of President Gorbachev himself, who showed up on the first day of the congress, a discussion of the proposed Union treaty was placed on the agenda. Evidently, the Gorbachevites had wanted to move quickly to adopt the treaty, but they didn't succeed in this. All of us regard Moscow with considerable apprehension, for it is there that the fate of the treaty will be decided and it is the Russian parliament that will ratify it, or not. It appears, however, that the servile terms of the treaty imposed by the center do not suit Russia either.

Kiev has its own distress, its own crisis. The "right" has chewed up the mayor who had emerged from among the democrats. Since his resignation, the city has been run by his deputy. The young physicist and Rukh activist Maksym Strikha, from whom I learn everything about what's going on in Kiev, is in a militantly pessimistic frame of mind: "It's all a mess, but we're not going to give in so easily."

Yesterday I visited Strikha's chaotic quarters, where a small group of us toasted the official registration of the Petro Mohyla Scientific Society, which is made up of a number of "young" (as we say) scholars. Strikha is in it, as are Hrytsenko, Zabuzhko, Riabchuk, Bilokin, and myself—all people you know. There are still other people, mainly computer programmers. Under the aegis of the Society, Bilokin is preparing the publication of a journal, *Nashe Mynule* (Our Past), and Hrytsenko, the annual "Who's Who in Ukraine." Such are the plans for the moment. I have no idea where the two of them expect to get paper. The paper situation at the state publishers is catastrophic. Dozens of books have disappeared from the publishers' plans for the upcoming year, since they have nothing on which to print them. There must be paper somewhere: a whole deluge of new newspapers with all kinds of views and tendencies has made its appearance. This is *the* sacramental question of our life: Where does everything vanish? And where does it come from? To which nobody has an answer.

They're debating the law on the police in parliament. About time, too. Kiev, like all other cities, is becoming dangerous to live in. Perhaps I seem like a petulant old woman, but I remember how pleasant and romantic it was to wander of an evening about the city, in the parks, especially in May, when everything was in bloom and perfuming the air. Nowadays this is dangerous entertainment. There is no peace of mind. There's always someone on the loose from prison; there's large-scale pilfering of weapons from the army; everyone's arming himself, and those who aren't doing so are trembling with fear.

Not long ago, before my very eyes, a nasty, dirty little fight broke out on the knoll near my apartment building. I was standing with Sasha Hrytsenko near the entrance to my building, on a respectable street near the university, when some guy ran up to us and spattered gas in our faces from a canister. Most of it fell on Hrytsenko, causing his eyes to tear. Fortunately, the gas didn't seem to be paralyzing; it was probably Soviet, for it did not produce the desired effect. Then this same guy realized he had made a mistake—that we were not the people he was after—and ran off. All this took seconds. He ran up to a group of three men not far off and they all broke into a brawl on the knoll. Later, from the balcony, I saw several more people from this company arrive on the scene. They all took off very suddenly, leaving behind them a body laid out on the road in the dark.

And recently a taxi driver (that typical Kievan taxi driver-type, belonging to the mafia, disheveled, at home in a shady world, the type who drives mafiosi around for big money, who trades hard currency, vodka and marijuana under the table, who knows the addresses of all the dens of iniquity), cordially informed me that he always packs a pistol on the night shift—for self-defence. "Wanna see it?" he asked.

December 4

The Great Council of Rukh met on Saturday, December 1, confirmed the new leadership, and worked out the tactics of the day. Rumors circulate that Rukh has employed one hundred people for its apparatus. This outrages some, who think there are too many new officials. Naturally, I was interested in the role of women in this new structure of Rukh. Women work at various kinds of secretarial jobs, they key in data, translate, and meet guests. All intellectual and political work goes to the men.

On December 1 and 2, the constituent assembly of the Party of Democratic Accord—the former Democratic Platform of the CPU—took place. Their group in the Supreme Rada numbers 22 people. They adopted their documents and took the name "Party of Democratic Renaissance of Ukraine."

Something quite serious has taken place in Moscow. On December 3, the RSFSR Congress of People's Deputies passed a law on the privatization of land in Russia. True, they forbade its resale for a ten-year period. Even such a half-measure was a blow to the partocrats, the Ukrainians among them. Our parliament is also discussing a land code and is spinning its wheels on this same question. The chairmen of the collective farms—our feudal princelings—and, naturally, the party bosses, who stand for the "socialist choice," or, as Lenin would have said, for their own class interests, are all desperately waging a struggle against the privatization of land. They've even hauled the Russian Orthodox church over to their side. One of the Ukrainian parliamentarians cited the opinion of the church which, apparently, has said that land comes from God and belongs to all; and so a single person cannot be in owner-ship of it. The ROC, as they say here, stands firmly on the platform of the CPSU.

No change in the Khmara story. Khmara is on hunger strike. Some of the deputies today wore white headbands themselves at the session of the Supreme Rada and the delegation from Lviv hung a protest sign right on the table. Should Khmara die—God forbid—there would be widespread disturbances in western Ukraine (young people there are already extremely hot-headed) and this could lead to unfore-seeable consequences, even to direct presidential rule in Ukraine. Khmara supporters are urging him to quit his hunger strike. But for the time being he holds stubbornly to his position.

D[mytro] P[avlychko] has returned from Vilnius where, on December 1, the three parliaments of the Baltic republics met in joint session. The Ukrainian opposition communicated its support to the Balts, who are girding themselves for the worst—the arrival of Soviet troops and civil disobedience. The Georgians are saying the same thing. Obviously we should be making similar preparations.

The Union treaty, i.e., its draft, hangs like the sword of Damocles. Yeltsin stated at his press conference that the Union center is appropriating too much for itself and that Russia will not give up its sovereignty. On the other hand, he continually affirms that a treaty is necessary.

I had a stormy discussion yesterday with D[mytro] P[avlychko]. I criticized the poster of the Republican Association of Ukrainists announcing the conference which is to take place in a couple of weeks. The poster features a blue background with yellow letters, and the acronym RAU appears in the shape of a trident. I said, perhaps too cuttingly (but in our debates we are both very cutting) that this poster signals that the conference—and scholarship itself—is to be patriotic, whereas in fact it must be objective, and the yellow-blue national colors and emblems have no obvious connection with scholarship. D[mytro] P[avlychko] thought otherwise. He thinks that all our conferences and congresses are not worth much on the whole (here he's not far from the truth, for the old scholarship is inadequate and the new has not yet emerged; there is only busywork), but on this occasion he also argued that if our fundamental political questions are not resolved, there will be no need for scholarship.

D[mytro] P[avlychko] is feeling deeply pessimistic, disillusioned by the apathy of a moribund people who don't deserve to have an independent state; by an opposition which is split over the Khmara affair (some consider it immoral to work in a parliament which permitted one of its deputies to be arrested; Iryna Kalynets demonstratively sits in the balcony and not at her seat, yet the secession of the democrats is exactly what the partocrats want); by the impulsive emotions of particular individuals. I caught this mood from him. We stopped quarreling and lapsed into melancholy.

Yet another problem that increasingly preoccupies me is my feeling about my personal status as a professional woman, and the attitude of particular male colleagues, and of society in general, toward it.

A year ago, our society didn't even know the word "feminism," but *perestroika*, people's travels to the West, and the broader exchange of information have all introduced it. Not long ago, I was talking with two of my male colleagues—men of my generation—about feminism. I got a bit carried away and started telling them about feminist theory, then happened to notice how they were exchanging condescending looks and laughing at me behind my back. As though to say, "Let her have her little say."

As a person acquainted with American culture, I absorbed these convictions step by step over a long period. True, even a couple of years ago I didn't attribute any particular significance to feminist theory or to my own feelings, which I would now formulate as the feelings of a woman in a hostile world. Now everything has changed dramatically, because all our society's painful problems, and this one too—the status of women—have spilled out into the open and become more acute. I have become exceedingly sensitive to how people treat me. Secondly, I am trying to impart a feminist awareness to my female colleagues, especially to those who have reached similar conclusions spontaneously and who now need a theoretical base.

But here everyone is always trying to convince us that our role is second-class and inferior, although this is objectively untrue.

The situation is made up of thousands of petty details.

For example, I drop by the ostentatious Presidium of the Academy. Our Academy is another of my morbid and painful subjects. A relic of feudalism, or a mixture of feudalism and socialism. I could go on for hours about its unfairness, the legalized parasitism of some of its members, and the absolute indifference to those who are actually getting some work done; about its utter contempt for the humanities.

So, the Presidium of the Academy. Hundreds of men—not scholars but paper-pushers, those who "organize" our scholars' work—rush about the corridors in deep concentration. At the entrance stands a policeman. You need a special pass to get in. Your ID as a member of one of the other academic institutes will not do. I walk in confidently so as not to be stopped by the policeman, who is too lazy to ask for the special pass. The ruse works.

At the office of one of the workers in the international department, I stand witness to a mortifying conversation. A respected academician is saying that a very solid and thoroughly perestroika-minded committee of scholars has been formed at a very high level and is headed up by the president of the Academy himself. What they need now is "some girl" who knows English and German, can translate and participate in negotiations with foreign scholars. He literally says, "some girl."

Everybody has long known that our male scholars don't know foreign languages; that it's mainly our female interpreters who know them—or, as we say here, the "girls," or "little girls." With such "girls" it is possible to be patronizing and supercilious, as though with support staff, except of a slightly higher class. No one feels uncomfortable about this; it's normal.

An incident from my life at the institute. One of our Doctors of Science, sheet of paper in hand, is running down the hallway when he meets a woman, a candidate of sciences and slightly younger than he, at the entrance. He asks her, "Can you type? It just so happens that I need...." It doesn't bother him in the least that he can't type a single page of text for himself; he doesn't notice that he addresses a younger woman familiarly while she speaks formally to him; he assumes it is absolutely normal that he, the "conceptualist," is the creative worker while someone else, usually a woman, is to serve him.

And if you could see the work of this conceptualist who, except for a few of the classics of Marxism and the Marxist philosophers published in the Russian language, has never read anything! Not because he didn't even want to, but because he never bothered to learn at least one foreign language.

Not long ago, a scene involving me and this same gentleman took place at a departmental meeting. I had contested the notion of another of our male colleagues, who had written that the "weak," female element, which has hindered the normal development of Ukrainian literature, must be rooted out. I received the reply: "And what in fact have women contributed to scholarship?" I was aghast at the proposed level of discussion. While I was recovering, I heard:

"I'll bring you a pamphlet where it is argued that feminism is a dead and passé theory which has accomplished nothing." Of course, the pamphlet is in Russian. I asked him if he'd read anything of the feminist theory or feminist literary criticism in English or French or any other foreign language. He replied in the negative. In other words, he's read nothing about feminism, but knows that it is frightful and simply inadmissible.

Similar incidents occur daily, almost by the minute. You're standing on the street with some male colleagues. Another man approaches. He shakes hands with everyone but you.

You criticize a male boss. He simply takes no notice and comments, "A woman doesn't know her own mind." This real instance happened to a friend of mine, a supremely thoughtful person, after which she went about for days feeling insulted and disillusioned.

And to read Ukrainian prose written by men, in which all the heroines dream of devoted service to the Male, or at least of attaining self-realization through love of him.

And to read Ukrainian poetry written by women, all of which says these same things.

And to look around you, where neither in the academic nor literary nor party nor ministerial leadership is there a single woman. None, anywhere.

I think I've already mentioned that I've written the Statute of the Women's Society of Rukh. Entirely in the feminist mode. They adopted it and even wanted to elect me president, but I declined. Numerous discussions on this theme took place between me and the activists of the Women's Society. Halyna Antoniuk, one of Rukh's elite, was sorry that I didn't want to lead the organization. I asked her, "And why don't *you* want to do it?" And she responded with complete sincerity that she had resolved never to get seriously involved in any women's organization. This is a typical point of view. Even women who are politically engaged and radically attuned consider women's affairs of secondary importance. They've accepted patriarchal clichés holus-bolus.

I've written before about the preparations for our feminist anthology. It's progressing slowly, for we lack theoretical background. We have organized a discussion circle with my colleagues Vira Ageieva, Natalka Shumylo, and Tamara Hundorova. The need for this anthology, as well as for a feminist conception at the foundation of our culture, is dawning on them. For each of them, as for me, this is a serious step on its own; it may even be considered an action, given the total negativism of our milieu. To be in an absolute minority and to feel this negativism isn't easy. Yet feminist studies and problems excite me all the more. I perceive a mountain of untouched subjects and possible projects, articles, books, conferences. You can see, more and more, how our culture is sick with sexism, with contempt for women, with the systemic division of roles and subordination of women, and with barbaric stereotypes.

The personal first fruits are already in: I have finished an article with the rather pompous title, "Between Feminism and Nationalism: New Women's Groups in Ukraine." For now in the English language for an English book.

December 9

If only you knew what a burden these letters have lately become!

What originated in my nostalgia for our Edmonton conversations and in my enthusiasm for the process of working on the computer, what has continued under pressure from you, is now much harder. In the first place, events are developing in such a way that I no longer feel like keeping track of them.

That is, on one hand, I enjoy following politics. There is this old Soviet game of the intelligentsia: to guess what's going to happen tomorrow; how a certain important figure is going to behave and how another will react. Moreover, now, as before, many events take place somewhere off-stage, in the wings, outside the purview of the newspapers and television. You can only speculate on what some periodic personnel changes mean. (For example, what is the significance of the recent appointment of General Gromov to the post of USSR deputy minister of the interior—only a rightward shift of the police or the neutralization of Gromov, distancing him from the army as a potential leader of a military coup? And so on.)

On the other hand, writing these letters is becoming much more onerous—if only because life here (and I mean political life) has, since spring, become markedly more intense and dramatic. Never before have things been as they are now in Ukraine. I'm quite aware that "important" history is being made, but it reminds me all the more of a storm in the northern seas that hurls one enormous iceberg against another. It's dangerous to be too close to these icebergs (although that doesn't concern me), and psychologically wearing. Putting out these fragmentary, spasmodic, sometimes even chaotic notes cum correspondence cum chronicle (if you're going to write in the heat of the moment, they can't come out any other way), I more than ever live through what's going on around me. And how I want to turn off the television when they broadcast the regular sessions of parliament! It's hard to bear when, before your eyes, everything's lurching to the right. I see it and understand it clearly, but at the same time I sense the mood around me or feel irritated by the indifference of others.

Besides, in writing these letters about what's going on, I am doomed to thinking always the same thoughts: Why is it like this? What for? And what next?

At our very occasional meetings, my mother-in-law, by the way, has been repeating lately, "They're going to arrest you! It's absolutely certain they're going to arrest you!" (After the war, her father was secretary of an oblast committee, and she received the appropriate training.) And I laugh, "Well, let them. There's no going back." And I say to myself, "Could it really happen?"

The political situation is becoming more aggravated and the political barometer is inching to the right. There's new confirmation of this. The other day, in Vinnytsia oblast, a democratic deputy of the Supreme Rada, Hudyma, was savagely beaten up. He was travelling with a group of eight in three cars. They were stopped in some village, dragged out of the cars and ferociously assaulted—obviously by plainclothesmen in full view of the passive villagers and policemen in uniform who, as is our custom, did not intervene. Hudyma is in hospital. On December 7, the democrats held a press conference at the Writers' Union. Today, in an official press communiqué, we were told that Hudyma had been making extremist statements in some village in Vinnytsia which had provoked the censure of the villagers, and that his injuries are second-degree.

Nor does the Khmara story inspire optimism. Yesterday, Kravchuk authorized four deputies to visit Khmara and to report to parliament on the state of his health. The group investigating the Khmara affair addressed Kravchuk later in the day, protesting the pressure exerted on the course of investigation.

Khmara isn't quitting his hunger strike, and they say he's worried that the entire nation has failed to rise in his defence. Parliament voted once again on the question of whether to release Khmara from jail, and a majority was once again against it. Moreover, the Procurator of the Ukrainian SSR, Potebenko, who wants to make of Khmara the biggest criminal in Ukraine, threatened another twenty-one deputies (who had made a statement about Potebenko's previous abuses of power) with criminal charges. And now we have also learned that a criminal charge has been laid against Oles Donii, one of the leaders of the student strike, for occupation of the university.

There was a rather feeble demonstration last Sunday in Kiev. Following on the officially approved rally in the square near the stadium, the crowd went on a "prohibited and illegal" march (as t.v. informed us) to Lukianiv prison, where Khmara is being held. On the whole, the people—that common, mythical people whom political opponents invoke against one another—is thinking about its daily bread or, at best, is following the course of events on television.

It's got cold in Kiev; snow is falling. Even the memorial service for the victims of the Tatar-Mongol invasion at the foundation stones of the Church of the Tithes (built by Prince Volodymyr) did not attract a great number of people. (Kiev was captured and destroyed by the Mongols on December 6,

1240.) Not even an announcement of free refreshments, courtesy of the city council, helped. There was no one to take the oranges and buns after the service.

This seems to be a new parenthesis of social lethargy—nobody cares about anything, some wonder how to survive, others how to get away. A handful of Don Quixotes want to change everything.

Last week the Supreme Rada passed the most contentious clause of the land code. Private ownership of land is not allowed. Rather, peasants are being given the right to use land in perpetuity, but prohibited from selling it. For the present, then, the conservatives prevail.

There was no session of parliament on Thursday, the 7th. The democrats walked out and thus there was no quorum. With the partocrats jeering at him, D[mytro] P[avlychko] made a statement in the name of the opposition, the Narodna Rada, about the Khmara affair.

D[mytro] P[avlychko]'s mood has become even blacker. The majority calls more and more loudly for new elections to the Presidium of the Supreme Rada, which is their way of getting rid of the opposition, D[mytro] P[avlychko] included. It looks as if Kravchuk is coming around to their point of view. The majority has also understood that the public doesn't give a damn (and maybe never will) and lets itself be wilfully disregarded. In the final instance, it demands something to eat, but nothing very special, anything will do. A while ago, we were discussing another scenario: they'll arrest a few dozen democrats and suspend the work of parliament at the same time. What will be the public's reaction? Except for the psychological shock and the revival of total terror, there probably won't be any reaction. A couple of thousand may take to the streets, but the rest will sit at home, waiting it out.

To conclude, something amusing. A couple of days ago, in *Vechirnii Kyiv*, I read the graphic announcement of a Kiev erotic (!) theater. They had placed a great number of titillating and very vulgar advertisements, at the center of which one reads the following aphorism: "Man's love is of man's life a thing apart; 'Tis woman's whole existence." Sure.

December 12

Yesterday at the usual time I went through a repeat of the same old story. Having put my daughter to bed, I trepidatiously turned on the television and, as though by design, came across the statement of the head of the USSR KGB, Kriuchkov, delivered, as he expressed it, on instructions from the President. In a rather slow and halting manner, he read about the upsurge of nationalists, separatists and all those whose ambition is the ruination of our state (the USSR). He particularly lingered over the subversive activities of the Western security services and those organizations which are conducting a clandestine war with us. How many times have we heard about all these enemies, internal and external! I remember how it all began with the announcement that such enemies were going to be ferreted out. Kriuchkov indicated that it would be impossible to "de-particize" his department (i.e., remove communist party cells), for this would not be consonant with human rights. His statement left me feeling thoroughly alarmed. All this has prodded me in the direction of an old theme: how hard it is to write these letters, because I don't want to read papers these days nor follow the news. It's too easy to ruin your mood and your nerves that way.

December 17

The second stage of the Communist party congress took place in Kiev on December 13-15. They mainly talked about Rukh, which has finally shown its "true" face, embracing terror (they were referring to the Khmara story); about extremists who want to wreck the "great state"; about how today's communists have nothing for which to apologize to the public, contrary to the demands of the democrats, and so on. Borys Oliinyk spoke in the same spirit, reaffirming the immortality of the communist idea. It all seems rather wearying and bleak.

Hurenko's report and the speeches that followed gave the

impression that time had stopped. It was impossible to understand just what year we were in: 1938, 1948 or 1990.

I have a friend—a musician graduated from the conservatory—who is a splendid example of a contemporary communist. Imagine a musician (the Kiev Conservatory still considers
music a category of ideology) who is at one and the same time
a singer in the Army chorus (its repertoire consists of communist songs about Komsomol volunteers from the time of the
civil war and recent songs in praise of our army) and a singer
in one of the church choirs in Kiev. He sings there every
Saturday, he makes the sign of the cross, kisses the priest's
hand and eats at the church dinners with devotion. With such
communists, it isn't communism you're building.

The constituent assembly of the Democratic party took
place on the 15th and 16th. This is the third Ukrainian party
which has the word "democratic" in its name. For the time
being, it's a party of the intelligentsia, but its program is highly
imposing: civil society, democracy, national accord. Debates are
waged among the democrats about why we create so many
parties. Our ruling party, i.e., the CPSU, has an interest in this
phenomenon, for it dissipates the forces of the opposition. But
the democrats are mutually irreconcilable. No one wants to
unite with anyone else. Yurii Badzio, who used to work in our
institute and who was later imprisoned for anti-Sovietism,
returning from internal exile only in 1988, was elected chairman of the Democratic party. Elected deputy chairmen were
my institute colleagues, Donchyk and Tsekov, and D[mytro]
P[avlychko] as well. Donchyk and Tsekov told me all about the
congress at work today. They are real enthusiasts who have
invested in the organization and congress and party an enormous amount of energy and personal effort.

Today, the 17th, the Third USSR Congress of People's
Deputies—which is to examine many questions, most important of which is the Union treaty—opened in Moscow. It began
with the proposal of a female deputy, elected to this body by
the CPSU, to place on the agenda the question of a vote of
non-confidence in the President. The reason: he had dismantled
the USSR—a great state. So, the right advances ever onward.

And yet, my first instinct was to wonder whether this proposal was not inspired by the President himself to give the democrats a good scare. The oppositional Inter-regional Group, which includes democrats from Ukraine, proposed withdrawing the question of the Union treaty from the agenda, cautioning the congress about a confrontation with the republics. In vain, of course.

December 26

Lately I've been following the peripeteia of political life less and less. I'm exhausted. Besides, the end of the year is approaching; without much enthusiasm I'm finishing up my work. I still have old obligations to discharge with several publishers: here an article, there an article. There's no time to be engaging in political intrigues and cataclysms. And, when cataclysm is a daily event, you stop seeing it as particularly urgent. Even the threat of a right-wing coup, because it's constant, has become humdrum.

A brief note about what's happening. The Moscow Congress of People's Deputies looks to be a complete failure. Gorbachev's report gave no hope for a way out from the crisis. The Union cracks and disintegrates, in spite of all efforts, within and without, to consolidate it. Shevardnadze's resignation has shaken everybody and raised a great hullabaloo. And the fact that the Congress resolved to keep the old name, USSR, personally shook me even more. Same for the resolution about the expedience of the Union treaty in the form proposed from above. Moreover, the army deputies demand ever more insistently that Gorbachev assume command of the army and restore order.

The West is graciously sending us Christmas presents; as we put it, "granting humanitarian aid." A lot is being said about this. On television they show our destitute elderly with milk or juice and Western goods. I read, in one of "your" papers, that the West is doing this in large measure to prop up Gorbachev. Among us there are several points of view on this aid, and many who condemn it. No matter how much you give an alcoholic to drink, he will never have enough. If the system is deficient, no amount of gifts or credit will help it.

The Supreme Rada has finished its session in Kiev. The budget for next year squeaked through. The right stuck to their positions throughout. In the "exchange of views" on the Union treaty, the partocrats were ready to sign anything; even Kravchuk was amazed. D[mytro] P[avlychko] tried to introduce a bill about the foreign-policy function of Ukraine, but even during the debate it was obvious the right was going to defeat it. So Kravchuk tabled it for some future date.

An unpleasant but symptomatic campaign has been initiated against D[mytro] P[avlychko]. *Radianska Ukraina* published a deeply offensive letter from some retired general accusing D[mytro] P[avlychko] of being a veteran of a certain well-known company of the Ukrainian Insurgent Army and demanding his recall from the Presidium of the Supreme Rada. Sympathizers have been phoning me for two days running, asking what they can do and how to react (D[mytro] P[avlychko]'s in Moscow attending the Congress of USSR People's Deputies). It's all very unpleasant and has left a bad taste in my mouth.

Today, adjourning its session, as a kind of bone tossed to the masses, the Supreme Rada confirmed Christmas, Easter and Whitsunday as national holidays.

We've had our successive large scholarly conference—this time the Republican Association of Ukrainists, which seems to have been more successful than all the preceding ones. The theme was very pertinent to today's situation—"Ukraine and Russia"—and there was less euphoria and hubbub at the meetings. Quite a few members of parliament showed up and some even gave speeches. Among these the most interesting was Hryniov, the deputy chairman of the Supreme Rada. He said that the opposition's favorite slogan, "No to the Union treaty!", was sterile, because in fact it provides no alternative to the Union treaty as proposed by Gorbachev, and the public can only rally around an explicitly positive program. Rukh also tried to organize a discussion on the treaty, and there was much polemic and various ideas but no consensus. There are alternative plans—perfectly decent ones—about a "Union" without a center. But I'll write about this, and other topics, in my next letter, for today I'm trying to get this letter off to you through some "good" people. So I'll break off here and wish you all the best.

December 31

In two hours it will be the New Year, but here I am with my, shall we say characteristic, eccentricity—even fanaticism (you see how much I've come under the influence of your idea of writing these letters!)—sitting at the table and tapping out the last jottings of 1990. The reason I refer to "eccentricity" is that, among us, it just isn't done to work on New Year's Eve. This has always been and still is our country's favorite holiday. Until this year, Christmas was celebrated as an illegal and clandestine festival. All others—November 7, May 1, Soviet Army Day, and the rest—are merely patriotic, official and soulless, whose only saving grace was that they meant a day off. But New Year's is truly a well-loved festival when, for one night, we are oblivious to the reality around us.

Thus I underscore my originality: everyone in the vicinity is drinking and dancing, while I, at 10:00 p.m., am sitting at my computer.

Honestly, though, I had reacted personally to the approaching holiday as though it were a divine punishment. My daughter had asked for a Christmas tree, some toys, gifts from Grandfather Frost or Santa Claus or St. Nicholas—it didn't matter from whom, just some presents, please! And where was I to get them when, by mid-December, all the stores were already empty? Thank heaven I managed to come upon an old, synthetic Christmas tree and last year's glass decorations. (I have always bought new ones, but not this year.) The Czech consul in Kiev rescued us, with a gift to D[mytro] P[avlychko] of a whole box of wonderful bonbons for the tree. So it all worked out.

As the New Year holiday was approaching, Kiev seemed anxious and overstrained as never before. The empty shops; prices at the farmers' market higher than even a week ago; the Caucasians who right between the meat counters at the Bessarabian Market offer you, from within their jackets, bottles of champagne at 50 rubles a crack (at least seven times dearer than the state price) for, on New Year's Eve, you absolutely must have champagne; the dark and gloomy streets; pathetic garlands in the empty shop windows; pictures of Sylvester Stallone in the kiosk windows alongside girlie calendars; newspapers, radio and television with news of the incessant political squabbling—none of this put one in a festive mood. But life goes on, people enjoy themselves as best they can, and try to forget themselves for at least one day and to have faith in something better.

I've had a good year. I'm really proud of the collection of T.S. Eliot's poetry that I edited-his first appearance in the Ukrainian language—and of my translation of D.H. Lawrence's *Lady Chatterley's Lover* for the first time into Ukrainian, ahead of the Russian translation and a *succès de scandale*; my foreword and commentary in the first Ukrainian edition of W.B. Yeats; and some other articles. Of course all this was translated and written some time ago, so now I'm simply reaping the fruits of earlier labors.

I did write some new things last year which are taking a long time to come out (you yourself know how long manuscripts languish at our publishers) or may never come out, given the severe paper crisis or Moscow's boycott of paper to Ukraine. Our publishers are on the verge of bankruptcy; they're letting staff go and cutting back drastically on their publishing plan.

But the most important thing that happened to me last year was that internal, personal transformation which I have been feeling. It's almost as though some new spirit or consciousness were living inside the old body. I have discovered myself irreconcilable to the world around me. My view on life has become sharper. "View" is exactly it—I notice things I did not notice before. I react strongly to things that formerly left me indifferent. At times I find "my" society utterly intolerable. The degraded state of Soviet academic scholarship, in which I, alas, still formally participate, is more and more irritating. My feminist enthusiasms cause me a lot of trouble. Some innocent, thoroughly unremarkable statement—for example, that a woman is a person, just like a man—provokes a storm of indignation in my immediate professional milieu. A few days ago, a very decent and quite sensible young poet said to me, "I didn't know you were a feminist. I used to have more respect for you." I myself don't know to what extent I am a feminist and what I can distill for myself from the various ideological strands of Western feminism. What I'll retain and what I'll discard. But the young man, who has no real understanding of feminism, already has "no respect" for me.

For all of us in this country, politics has become a total obsession, a mania, a narcotic. From the janitor to the academician. Like true fanatics, we all put other business aside to rush to the television set and watch the first broadcasts from our first parliaments. We began and ended our day with conversations about who will be elected, who appointed, what so-and-so said, what so-and-so answered. Nor was I exempt from this passion.

I experienced some extraordinary moments last year. Having become one with the demonstration of September 30, about which I wrote you, I felt for the first time the potential strength of thousands and thousands of people around me, felt the stirrings of this people, felt that the injustices of history may yet be repaired and its iron logic shattered—as in the victory of the students in October.

At the same time, as never before, in 1990 I succumbed to attacks of pessimism, thinking of our domestic woes—Chernobyl, our fearsome and mendacious system which turns people into cripples, the total brutalization and dehumanization of life. And, although I live in exceptionally good circumstances—as far as local conditions go—and mingle not with the "working people" but with intellectuals, poets, and theoreticians in various fields—from versification to management—nevertheless I see and understand it all quite well! That is, I see how everything is bad and becoming worse, and harder. Thus, the end-of-the-year counters of Kiev force me to think of hunger (earlier, I would simply not have believed such a thing) and the endless, closely packed queues of wan, exhausted people in the suffocating grocery shops lined up for sausage (which turns blue when exposed to the air) or butter once more convinced me how terrible is the abyss of disrespect for each other at which we have arrived after these 73, now 74, malignant years.

So, a year has gone, flown by, and what an incredible number of things have happened in Ukraine, in Kiev, in the USSR. It's hard to know how to sum it up: what seems important today may be forgotten in a year, let alone in ten. But it is certain that a decade from now the year 1990 will still be seen as a notable one in Ukrainian history. And there'll be more than one dissertation about it written by my colleagues. (It's going to be interesting to read them eventually.)

We have moved forward at an unbelievable rate, and much of what seemed unimaginable even a year ago has come true: the blue-and-yellow flags fluttering over our cities, democratic councils in western Ukraine, the declaration of sovereignty, the accords between Russia and Ukraine. Political prisoners have become members of parliament.

At the same time, all these triumphs have failed to satisfy us; on the contrary, they have brought us overwhelming, all-consuming disappointment: the more you have, the more you want. We have all understood how far we still have to go to attain democracy, freedom of expression, freedom in general. And well-being? Now there's something quite unimaginable! This disappointment has laid a shadow across our whole life, on every conversation; it's in people's gestures and pantomime; it is within me: I feel it almost biologically, as something which is always just *there* and cannot be shaken off.

I don't know whether it's possible to fashion some more-or-less systematic idea of the past year from my letters. I wrote only about what I myself saw or heard, without going into analysis. Sometimes I didn't get around to noting down something important—I didn't have the time or energy—and by the next day the perception had faded. These are the real gaps, the "blank spots."

The resurgent "right," which gained ascendancy late in the year, obscured the "great" gains of the preceding months. The same people who voted in the summer "for" Ukrainian sovereignty, in December were voting "against." Some dual deputies—i.e., of the USSR and the Ukrainian SSR—voted for the acceptance of the Declaration of Sovereignty of Ukraine on June 16, and in December against the resolution proposed to the Third Congress of People's Deputies by the Inter-regional Group on the recognition of the sovereignty of the republics. Such inconsistency shook up a lot of people, though perhaps it's only logical, given our system. Voting against the recognition of republican sovereignty were Oliinyk and the president of our Ukrainian Academy, Paton. And Khmara is still in prison. If one considers our state, of which, it seems, only the enigmatic name has remained, no word of which corresponds to reality (What's the Union? What's socialism? What's soviet? Maybe you, a political scientist, know something?), then the crisis between the center and the republics has become acute in the extreme. In essence, the center does not recognize our sovereignty, and the republics—most particularly Russia—are not prepared to give up so easily. But the "right" is consolidating itself and is threatening us with the consequences. And we in reply flippantly joke about Magadan and Kolyma.

On central television three days ago, the most popular Soviet program, the news magazine *Vzgliad*, was banned for the simple reason that its hosts intended to speak about the resignation of Eduard Shevardnadze. In Ukraine, unrest is rampant. The local rightists, probably in co-ordination with their Moscow colleagues, are pressing in from all sides. It looks as if the democrats are afraid of a referendum on the Union treaty in its Gorbachev version. There's little chance of a majority voting against the treaty. But the machine just keeps on rolling, every day some "party" work is undertaken, the democrats try to regroup, to build some new blocs and consolidate new parties.

My parents dropped by today and D[mytro] P[avlychko],

however surprising it may be, was in a rather optimistic frame of mind for the first time in a long while. If you can call it optimism. He considers it most important not to yield one's ground, to work toward the supreme goal, which still lies far ahead—perhaps ten, perhaps twenty, perhaps even thirty years hence—but Ukraine will gain its liberty all the same. Maybe my little Bohdanna will be the only one to live to see it. To tell you the truth, this sort of optimism does little for me.

Now and then there's even something to chuckle about. For example, the last bit of business of the democrats in Ternopil was to cancel the New Year holiday, because it fell during the pre-Christmas fast and, naturally, all democrats and true Ukrainians would be fasting....

In a couple of minutes just before midnight, any minute now, Gorbachev will appear on television and say something to the people about *perestroika*.

Today's *Vechirnii Kyiv* printed a nice little joke about him: "On the news tonight:

At Last Harvest Collective Farm they are preparing to meet our head of state. The cortege drives up; the head of state steps out and addresses the crowd.

'How are you?'

'Very well,' the people reply.

'You're going to be living even better!' the General Secretary responds, joke for joke."

January 7, 1991

Today is Orthodox Christmas, probably the first normal Christmas holiday since the Revolution. A lot of people in Kiev don't have any idea what kind of festival it is, or how to mark the occasion. Crowds of people are attending full-length services in the churches, and on Khreshchatyk there were real Christmas pageants, quite witty and up-to-date. In one, King Herod resembled Gorbachev and, when his soul descended to Hell, he promised not the sign the Union treaty. It's a good thing that, in all this glumness around here, people have retained their usual sense of humor.

In his New Year's message, with which I ended my last letter, the GenSec [General Secretary] was very cautious and said nothing new. But what could he say, considering that in March it will be six years since he came to power and everything around us is chaos and ruin?

Personally, I have cooled off somewhat to politics and am relieved that parliament's on holiday recess and nothing's going on there. I've retreated into my own "space" and am enthusiastically reading Simone de Beauvoir and other feminist classics, inspired as I am to be doing my own women's studies. I've been writing easily and well these last several days. Yet another paradox.

Here's an interesting story, typical of our times. A friend of my sister's has left her husband because he's a hardline communist, and she herself has joined the Democratic party. This party has opened its headquarters in the department of literary theory at our institute. My departmental colleague, Yurii Tsekov, deputy head of the party, is busy working on its structure, recruitment and grass-roots organization. Almost daily, people wanting to join the party or to organize entire new cells come by to see him. And the other day I found Yurii Badzio, the party head himself, thin, worn out by prison and tuberculosis, seated at my desk. I often look at him and wonder how he endured all those years of prison and exile. You could not find anywhere a kinder, gentler, more intelligent person, a man seemingly incapable of any rudeness.

January 12

A war with Iraq could break out soon. I look for even the smallest bit of news on the subject in our papers. I think constantly of my numerous friends and acquaintances who are now in Israel. My Bohdanna, who isn't even four years old yet, really startled me today when, for the nth time, she asked me why Vitia Kagan no longer comes to see us. (He's a good friend of ours who left for Israel a year ago.) And when I started to explain that he is now living far away, in another country, she burst into tears, as only children do, utterly inconsolable, and said, "They're going to kill him there!" Absolutely amazed, I asked her why. And she answered, "There's a war going on over there." I felt as if she had reached in and squeezed my heart. Because it could be true, and because her little child's heart already knows such suffering.

The conflict in the Persian Gulf worries us most of all who understand that this would be a convenient time for some kind of right-wing coup. But the most awful thing is that there are people who consider Hussein a hero and the only person capable of standing up to the U.S. There are even those who would not mind fighting on his side.

But there are concrete fears close to home.

Some days ago, additional special forces were sent into the Baltic states, Moldova and Ukraine, ostensibly to check on last year's autumn call-up into the Soviet army. The situation in the Baltics is tense, because the call-up was only minimally fulfilled there. On today's morning news they showed tanks in the streets of Vilnius, ostensibly guarding the press building and the local DOSAAF (All-Union Voluntary Society for Assistance to the Army, Air Force and Navy of the USSR).

It's not as bad as that here, but a quiet panic is palpable nevertheless. Hryniov, Kravchuk's deputy, spoke on television on the 10th and said that, in his view, what's behind the introduction of the additional military contingents isn't any grand political strategy, but simply the panicky reaction of the center, which can no longer keep the machinery of the USSR under control. However, there are some deputies of the USSR—officers and Col. Alksnis—who say openly that, in order to improve the economy, a state of emergency must be declared and Gorbachev as well as Yeltsin must be removed. I read this in *Komsomolskaia Pravda*. Now I know what "glasnost" is. It's learning about a coup not from the sight of tanks in the street but from reading about it two weeks in advance in the newspapers.

Also on the 10th, Khmara's lawyers held a press conference at the Writers' Union. The trial hasn't started yet, but the outlook is disquieting. They've drawn up a whole bunch of absurd accusations against him, some of which carry a sentence of fifteen years (e.g., the theft of Col. Hryhoriev's wallet, which had been returned to him immediately, or robbery—damage to colonel's shirt and belt).

Also arrested is Oles Donii, leader of the Kiev Ukrainian Students' Union and of the October student strike, charged with occupation of the university. Other participants are being summoned one by one for interrogation at the procurator's. We all had a presentiment of this arrest, but our repressive system bided its time until the beginning of exams and vacation, when classes are no longer in session and students can't organize. The Students' Union leaders declare that they're going to defend Donii and struggle with every means at their disposal. It's possible that a new strike wave is imminent. Donii spoke to the Supreme Rada in October, presenting the students' demands. He was such a strange and unexpected sight at the podium of our parliament with his punk hairdo—long white strips of hair hanging from the back of his head. He called Kravchuk, very amusingly, very inapropos, "Mr. Leonid." Then Kravchuk promised that there would be no persecution of the participants in the student movements. Now Oles Donii is in jail and, as our press has informed us, "nationalist" literature was found in his apartment. It's been quite a while since we've heard that term.

The democrats, it seems, have been thrown into confusion. Chornovil, who not so long ago spoke out against strikes, now calls for a warning strike in defense of Khmara. Oles Shevchenko is proposing the convening of an extraordinary session of parliament, but what would that accomplish, given that parliament has already taken a vote on Khmara's account several times and each time the majority has voted to keep him in jail?

Yesterday there was a celebratory meeting of the Academic Council at our institute. We were celebrating the eightieth birthday of our colleague, Stepan Andriiovych Kryzhanivsky. He's one of the founders of the theory of socialist realism in its

Ukrainian version, a Komsomol poet of the '30s, probably the last living author of the collective poem of the '30s, "Ode to the Great Stalin from the Ukrainian People." The celebration turned out quite surrealistic. Imagine our hall with its cold blue walls. In a corner, a kitschy plaster bust of Shevchenko. On the wall behind the table (where our tripartite directorship is seated), an even kitschier metallic bas-relief of Lenin who, as we all know, never had anything to do with our institute or with Ukrainian literary studies. That bas-relief has been hanging there some thirty years; nobody takes any notice of it any more, but neither have they taken it down. At a large table are seated the members of the Academic Council—our geriatric patriarchs. Somehow or other, two years ago, I was elected to this company, to make it more "youthful." But I am not seated with them; like a "dissident," I sit with the people in the hall.

Our director, who is secretly awaiting the return of the Bolsheviks, announced in a monotonous voice with theatrical caesuras that "Today we have gathered together to mark the birthday of our colleague.... He has now attained the age of..." he paused, and someone in the hall, quietly but so that everyone could hear, said, "a hundred years." From everyone a strangled guffaw. Then another speaker spoke of our honored guest's merits, addressing him where he sat in the hall: "You created and laid the groundwork for the theory of socialist realism...." Our younger people exchanged glances and began whispering audibly to each other: "Great merit like hell! The theory of socialist realism is just the theory of party loyalty, folk worship and other such principles thanks to which our literature was almost wiped out in certain periods of not-so-ancient history." And yet we thank him amiably, this old man, so quiet and well-meaning, a humorist and bon vivant who just recently remarried yet again.... Sometimes it occurs to me that, if I were simply to describe our institute—what it's like, how it functions, how it gets along—not even a Beckett or an Ionesco could rival it for theater of the absurd.

In the evening, on the way home, I ran into my former Ukrainian language and literature teacher. She's already a pensioner and lives nearby, just around the corner. She clutched my hand, obviously disturbed.

"What's going to happen? Are they going to arrest us all?"

And I said, "Not you, of course, but us, maybe."

Another striking story in my life is connected with this same teacher. In the style typical of our educational system—a style to set your teeth on edge—our teacher compelled us to memorize dozens of poems. While we were studying Shevchenko, she gave us homework every day: to learn yet another poem. In class, she called us all in turn, one after the other, up to the blackboard for the recitation. I will never in my whole life forget the awful mindlessness of standing by that board and idiotically reciting those poems for her evaluation. Because of that teaching method, there were a lot of my classmates who ended up loathing Shevchenko and Ukrainian literature, even though our teacher had only wanted, by this means, to make us into little patriots.

(That school was special. Founded in the 1870s as a college, it functioned for several decades as an establishment for the elite. Many famous people studied there. When I was there, there were students in every class whose parents were in jail as prisoners of conscience and, at the same time, in every class there were children of well-known official writers and intellectuals—the elite, it would seem, but one that our society never trusted. But everything in this school—both teachers and students—was "under cover," i.e., under strict supervision. As a result, in 1976 they shut our school down, and my class was the last to finish there. Even today, though, among graduates of various years and eras there exists something on the order of a fellowship or solidarity.)

But to get back to our teacher. When her own grandchildren were growing up (sometime at the beginning of the 1980s), she sent them off to a privileged Russian-language school where, at that time, the wife of the late Shcherbytsky was on staff, teaching the children of the nomenklatura. When I heard about this, I was shocked. I couldn't contain myself, and the next time I met her I asked, "Why?" She began to mutter something by way of excuse, saying that the school was closer to home and had good teachers. And I, former teacher's pet, did not forgive her something I couldn't even find a name for.

What was it—Ukrainian hypocrisy, opportunism, conformism, the Ukrainian tragedy? I don't know. But even now this incidental little story still hurts and aggrieves me.

January 14

Terrible things have been happening in the last two days. In Lithuania, innocent people have been killed; tanks and Soviet soldiers are patrolling the streets of the Lithuanian cities. A punitive expedition of the empire, or center, of which we all had a presentiment that we didn't want to credit, has begun. There are barricades in the streets of Riga and Tallin. The people are preparing to defend their parliaments. Like many others, I utterly loathe this evil system, but feel at the same time the grievous weight of my own powerlessness.

Gorbachev spoke today in the Supreme Soviet of the USSR about the deadlock, the unconstitutional nature of Lithuania's acts of parliament, about the telegrams from workers sent to Moscow pleading for protection against local nationalists in the government, and a lot of other cynical things. He said he had not given the order to shoot and had only learned of the incident early this morning. He's shifted all the blame onto the Lithuanian parliament. Yeltsin, who was in Lithuania yesterday, declared that this was an attack on democracy in general. Who knows but that tomorrow something like it will happen somewhere else. In Kiev and Moscow yesterday, there were spontaneous, unauthorized rallies protesting the conduct of the soldiers.

Television, which became, literally overnight, as reactionary as in the time of Brezhnev, is broadcasting only official information. Moreover, they have programmed a whole series of mindless shows, some endless concerts, old film comedies; anything that's political, especially from an independent perspective, has disappeared or been yanked off the air. Once again we have to tune into radio stations from the West in order to find out anything at all.

Yesterday I was out at the dacha with my parents. We got together to celebrate the Old Style (Julian calendar) New Year—D[mytro] P[avlychko]'s favorite holiday. It was a disaster. We were too preoccupied with worry. And at night I couldn't sleep. I was suddenly prostrated by fear—cosmic and yet totally concrete. Our dacha is in the woods. At this time of year, the neighboring buildings are empty. I remembered the recent threats against D[mytro] P[avlychko]....

And today, at work, we marked the Old Style New Year in the department at the Institute of Literature. We gathered and stood around, wordlessly drinking to the memory of the fallen. It wasn't a party but a funeral. We are under a cloud of pain and anxiety. Rumors are circulating about some serious problems at the Chernobyl atomic energy station. And Khmara and Donii are still in jail.

January 16

Yesterday and today, with all our attention focused on Lithuania and the Baltics, everyone's been discussing the reaction of the West. Thus, in the Lithuanian paper, *Respublika*, there appeared an article under the headline, "Thanks, gentlemen, but it's already too late." A delegation from the Kiev city council and the Supreme Rada travelled to attend the funeral of the victims. Even the Presidium of our Supreme Rada issued a unanimous statement of alarm and protest.

Everyone blames the center, but the center won't budge. Television today broadcast a totally chauvinistic film about the special forces in Lithuania, who announced that they had come to defend to the death the television station and the local Soviet police academy in Vilnius against the troops of Sajudis, the popular movement.

Yesterday a group of our young writers and literary scholars—essentially those who had gone to the square in October in support of the students—got together at the Writers' Union.

Myself included, of course. We drew up a statement in the name of the ad hoc committee formed defend Oles Donii and are sending it to the Supreme Rada and to all the papers. Who knows whether it will do any good. And we still don't know who gave the go-ahead for the arrest, since Kravchuk made an official promise not to persecute the students.

January 22

With the launch of the Gulf war on the night of January 17, I can imagine how American television is presenting it. Our own media are showing quite a lot of it. On hearing the news about the strikes against Israel, I froze: I have countless friends, former Kievans, who now live in Haifa. Fear of radiation and disillusionment with our system drove many away from here and now, in their new land, they have to wear gas masks.

When I left work on the 18th, I saw a demonstration of Arab and Cuban students near city council. One hundred and fifty men with Iraqi flags, and the slogan, "Hands off Iraq!" Most interesting was that they stood on the steps and yelled, "Down with Bush!" in the Ukrainian language! The fruits of Ukrainization....

Everyone is still in a state of shock from the events in Lithuania. It's obvious that this was a planned coup d'état that didn't come off. It was supposed to result in a takeover of power by the mysterious Committee of National Salvation. We don't know its composition, but liaison with it is maintained by the Central Committee of the Lithuanian Communist party. Official information, being censored, is very limited, but it's clear that we were teetering on the brink of a really dangerous situation. While we all wondered who would be next, yesterday's events answered our question: at night, in Riga, people once again were dying at the hands of the Special Forces, this time mainly journalists.

By Monday morning, all of Kiev, and probably the whole of the Soviet Union, knew about the seizure of the Latvian Interior Ministry by the Special Forces. Just yesterday there were demonstrations in Moscow, Leningrad and Kiev in support of Lithuania, and now...Riga. I heard about it on the street this morning from my colleague Tolia Shpytal, who knows the Latvian language and was listening to Latvian radio all night. My head is hammering from pain and horror. How can one live in this empire of evil? In this perpetual mourning?

On March 17, the entire population of the Union is going to be voting for or against the expediency of its preservation. I refer to the so-called all-people's referendum. The question has been formulated in a very leading manner: "Do you consider essential the preservation of the Union of Soviet Socialist Republics as a renewed federation of equal and sovereign republics in which the rights and freedoms of individuals of every nationality will be fully guaranteed?" There's a lot of discussion among us about the contradictions within the question itself: preservation and renewal, for example.

In the meantime, on the 20th, there was a referendum in the Crimea about the creation of an autonomous Crimea as part of Ukraine. Just as we expected, the overwhelming majority voted for autonomy. Only the Tatars, who want their own national autonomy, were opposed, but they're in the minority, in no position to decide anything.

And now, to everyone's amazement, they've released Donii from jail. Khmara, of course, remains inside.

On Sunday, in spite of the cold, some 20,000 people gathered in St. Sophia's Cathedral Square to mark the anniversary of the union of the Ukrainian National Republic[45] with the Western Ukrainian National Republic, the day of Ukrainian unification. After the rally and the prayer service, the demonstrators moved on to the former building of the Central Rada and the Shevchenko monument.

Yesterday there was a literary evening with D[mytro] P[avlychko]. There was a horde of people in the large theater and even more outside it who hadn't been able to get tickets. It was hard to tell whether they came for poetry or politics. I'd guess mainly for politics.

January 27

Today's a regular "holiday." The day of the Central Rada's rout of the January uprising at the Arsenal factory in Kiev. That was in 1918. It's a communist celebration because, as official historiography has it, the uprising was revolutionary, while the Central Rada was bourgeois and counter-revolutionary. Probably that's why they're selling real barbecued meat and beer without coupons near the Arsenal today. Otherwise there wouldn't be enough of the brand-new Bolsheviks to observe this communist holiday.

Reaction is getting the upper hand in our country as every day brings another presidential decree. The most disagreeable one concerns the exchange of banknotes of 50 and 100 rubles in a three-day period, from the 23rd to the 25th. This provoked an unbelievable panic. The unfortunate pensioners and invalids, who were permitted to exchange only 200 rubles, jammed together in queues at the savings banks. Most of them stored their money at home, because old folks just don't trust the state. They were having heart attacks right at the cashiers' wickets, someone was crushed by the crowd, and so on. And at the markets speculators sold 100-ruble banknotes for 25. On the last day, traders in lemons from the Caucasus at the Bessarabian Market were selling 100-ruble notes for 5. And the big mafiosi, against whom this measure was apparently directed (so the democratic press tells us), only laughed, for they had either changed their money or put it into real estate long ago. Obsessed for three days by what to do with their money, no one got any work done. Prices on the black market—so far the only one—immediately jumped, and economists predict that inflation will increase even more, for the state, instead of keeping the old currency in circulation, is printing up new money—and that is the extent of its financial radicalism.

There was a localized panic in Kiev yesterday. Hearing rumors that the level of radioactivity in the water in the cooling pond at the Chernobyl atomic energy station had risen, and, in a flood, radioactive water would reach the Dnieper, the city's source of drinking water, the three millions of us Kievans spent the whole night on the phone, cautioning each one another to stock up on water. Absurd advice, because, if something like that did occur, no amount of water in reserve would help. And so we passed a nightmarish night, the phone ringing ceaselessly. Next day the radio and television notified us that it had been a false alarm, but by then our nerves were shot. As in the case of the money, for a long time now no one has believed the bureaucrats who reassure us that everything's fine and for the best.

Yesterday's evening news surpassed even that about the exchange of banknotes. It concerned the promulgation of a decree (which, it turned out, had been signed earlier) from two Union ministries, Defense and Interior, to the effect that, as of February 1, the streets of the larger cities and the capitals of the Union republics will be patrolled by armed military detachments (with armored vehicles, as required), as well as by the police. The democratic press and democratic municipalities have protested; the public (those who are capable of understanding the import of all this) is appalled.

Yesterday, the last remaining "left-wing" television program, initiated a couple of years ago as infotainment, showed us that notorious film sequence from Vilnius of the tanks dispersing the people and the machine gunners firing into the crowd. (The whole world—except us, naturally—has already seen it.) I didn't even realize that, at the end of the broadcast, sitting stunned in front of the t.v. set, I was weeping. I tell you honestly that this has never happened to me before. I've already written to you about this, but I repeat it over and over: the powerless hatred toward this iniquitous system—this heavy, heavy powerlessness—simply harrows and crushes you.

February 1

Today was to have been a special day. The beginning of quasi-martial law, which six republics have officially protested. Ukraine has not yet offered any official reaction, but some deputies have given an interview, saying that military patrols would be for our own benefit. While they were being interviewed, we awaited with great interest the arrival of military patrols with automatic weapons and armored cars in our streets. But everything seems quiet in Kiev. I hear that the city council is preparing a special resolution which will prohibit such patrols on the territory of Kiev. It's been freezing here the last few days. Outside it's sunny, windy, and 20 below. My fantasies have lately taken on a surreal quality, and so I sit and wonder whether it's cold inside a tank in such weather.

There's chaos at home: the child is sick, her cold turned into bronchitis. I can't seem to cure her horrible cough, and it makes me nervous that I don't have proper medicines (and I think of Canadian pharmacies...).

I left her for a couple of hours today and, showing up at work around lunchtime, heard some more surrealistic news. At ten in the morning, the academic secretary of the Institute had walked through the offices, checking whether his co-workers were present. An hour later, there hung an order on the board near the director's office that all "offenders against discipline" are to write explanatory notes to the director accounting for their absence. Once again, our directors are pretending not to notice that, in our institute, there is simply nowhere to work; that there are ten people to each room; and that our job doesn't involve sitting behind desks, but writing scholarly works. The last of such inspections had taken place long ago, before the time of "perestroika." For the rest of the day there was a great deal of discussion in the corridors about the inspection. "How easily everything slips back!" intoned our local democrats, like a refrain.

Everyone knew that the inspection was carried out in order to provide an incontrovertible, formal pretext for punishment, if it were to become necessary. If it were a case of the directors' checking the quality and level of our written work, that would be understandable, but this has never been done, for our director does not, himself, write anything.

Today we put our signatures to yet another protest letter against the decree concerning military patrols. And again there were those who refused to sign.

Our Ukrainian parliament opened its third session today. It will continue into June and is to adopt some one hundred laws, although the deputies themselves raised the reasonable question of who needs all these laws when the President of the USSR, with a single decree, can annul them. The polarization of society continues. It's especially obvious in the press: some papers have clammed up and write about nothing of particular importance, while others have moved ahead. Those which have remained democratic speak even harsher truths. For example, *Moscow News* was recently criticized by Gorbachev. The "right" isn't wasting any time either. Yesterday, at the Plenum of the Central Committee of the CPSU in Moscow, someone said that the party must go on the offensive. You might say it's already done so, judging from the blood spilled in Vilnius and Riga.

As you see, the confrontation of political forces continues unabated, which means that everything happens in waves here, with many repetitions. The constant repetition and running in place are enervating, and I know people who have stopped reading the papers, preferring to be ignorant of everything that's going on in the various Supreme Soviets.

Many truly interesting changes are taking place in our artistic and intellectual circles, where I truly have my being. Fine books are being published, original plays are being produced, really excellent exhibitions and whole new art galleries are opening. In literary life, there are new groups, tendencies, and names. The new, young writers are simply glutted with the intellectual and aesthetic freedom that their older colleagues never enjoyed. That feeling of being provincial and second-rate, with the everlasting orientation on Moscow— to publish in Moscow, to make an appearance in Moscow, to write as they do in Moscow, to be praised by the Moscow critics: such was the acme of fulfillment for the writer from the republics not so long ago—has vanished from our psychology. Although the writing life has become very difficult, and there's nowhere to publish, paper has become very dear and so on, nevertheless it is a free, unfettered and sane life as never before.

A youth subculture is evolving at a furious rate. Rock music didn't exist in Ukraine two or three years ago (while a music underground definitely existed, officially rock had no status, much less Ukrainian rock), but now there's good jazz and rock, on cheap, homemade instruments; poets experiment with texts, often of a political character, and composers with music. Our own Ukrainian rock stars are appearing, as is "popsa," a sentimental, primitive disco music, along with lots of other things.

It's very pleasant to be able to write when everything is permitted, even if, in the midst of it, there's nothing to eat. And even though they're not very happy about putting the new music on television, and the magazines and publishing houses do not readily publish the new poetry and stories, nevertheless freedom is the sweetest thing, especially for those of us who know what it is not to have it. And even if someone should try to ban something, they will not be able to take away our inner freedom.

You see, I, too, can be optimistic.

March 20 - 25

It's been more than two weeks since my last letter. I'm beginning to feel that I'm unable to keep up this chronicle. In my last letters, I've been straying from the general, social cataclysms to my personal affairs and problems. And there's so much political news every day that you could spend the whole day writing about it and analyzing it. I'm not saying that I'm bored by it, but I'm convinced that I've exhausted my capacity at this stage.

The all-Union referendum, which was held on March 17, completed another historical stage or, rather, a little shuffle. You can put a period after it, or, more precisely, an ellipsis. Although six years have passed since the beginning of "perestroika," we continue to live completely ignorant of what will happen on the morrow.

So, I'm writing you my last letter, and at the same time an

epilogue to the previous letters.

I had a wonderful time in Toronto and took part in one more academic conference dedicated to the politics of "glasnost." I returned home two days after the "notable" political event, the first in our history, etc., etc., as our official press described it: the March 17 referendum.

I was greeted on my return to Kiev by a blast of winter and a diphtheria epidemic. People were discussing the still incomplete data of the referendum results and the coal miners' strikes in full swing throughout the Union, including the Donbas. Among the strikers' political demands is the resignation of President Gorbachev and the transfer of power to the Council of the Federation, i.e., to the fifteen leaders of the Union republics. Among the demands of the Ukrainian strikers is the full constitutional ratification of the declaration of state sovereignty of Ukraine.

Also, while I was away the government announced a colossal rise in prices as of April 2. At last, what people here have most feared will come to pass. There's no point in going to the shops: they are definitively and irreversibly empty. Our mendacious Union government swore six months ago that it would be absurd to introduce market relations with a price rise. Now it's a fait accompli. As always, there are monopolistic, uniform prices imposed on everyone from above, from Ukraine to Turkmenia.

During my absence from the institute, our Marxist director retired. The smallest triviality testifies to the epochal change, and we observe it as only fitting.

Naturally, the recent referendum is the most intriguing topic. It's interesting that both sides (Gorbachev as well as his political opponents) declared a victory. Just as the referendum changed nothing and won't change anything and *could* not have changed anything at this stage, so it has not rescued our doomed and tormented Union. The republics, with the exception, perhaps, of the Central Asian ones, will be in no hurry to sign the Union treaty as originally proposed, formulated as it was in such a colonialist and enfettering manner. That much is now clear.

Six months ago I thought that, should the majority say "yes" to the Union, I'd interpret this as a personal as well as national catastrophe. Well, it happened. Nearly 70 % voted for the Union. As you see, I am still alive. And not feeling it to be such a fatal thing as I had thought I would, six months ago. I even have a bit more optimism. After all, you can't really consider this a true victory for the Center. Six republics (Estonia, Lithuania, Latvia, Moldova, Georgia and Armenia) didn't participate in the referendum at all and, in those republics which did vote, millions of people didn't go to the polls. In fact, only a little more than half the citizens of the Union who had the right to vote voted "for."

Same thing in Ukraine. Almost 70% for, 30% against. Of those who voted. If you include the non-voters, then the Union supporters are a bare majority (58%). The results of the vote in Kiev shook everybody. Only 44% said "yes" to the Union. Kiev, like Sverdlovsk, Yeltsin's home town in Russia, has turned out to be a city of decided separatists. That's something to think about.

The Supreme Rada of Ukraine managed to come to a decision on the holding of its own republican referendum with its own question: "Do you agree that Ukraine should be included in a Union of Soviet Sovereign States on the basis of the declaration of state sovereignty of Ukraine?" The leaders of the democratic movement and of the parliamentary opposition differed in their attitude toward it. The Galicians agitated against any sort of union, while others considered this a serious political miscalculation. And yet the "yes" vote exceeded all expectations—more than 80%. Parliament has received nation-wide support for the declaration.

In three western Ukrainian oblasts, they conducted their own, Galician referendum as well, with a question analogous to the one asked in the recent Lithuanian referendum: "Do you want Ukraine to be an independent state with autonomy to decide all questions of internal and external policy and to guarantee equal rights for all citizens irrespective of national or religious affiliation?" An overwhelming majority, more than 80%, responded "yes."

But most interesting is the fact that the positive results (for the Center) of the March 17 referendum have, in principle, decided nothing regarding the fate of the republics, ours included. It's bought some more time for Gorbachev. And, for Yeltsin, a victory: in the Russian republican referendum, 80% voted for the direct election of the Russian president.

The Ukrainian parliament is engrossed in drafting and passing laws—on enterprises, state customs duties, the status of citizens who have suffered from the effects of the accident at Chernobyl, etc., etc. Even in the dreadful polemics and the political struggle between independentists and partocrats, the process of state-building is going on. This is, by and large, impressive. Sometimes the parliamentary debates might seem unprofessional, futile, even comical, and, for most people, obscure. But even the most skeptical person must acknowledge this slow-paced, steady *forward* motion. Motion which is likely unstoppable. Or very difficult to stop. In this slow motion you can see the first model of our near future.

This is quite pleasing, although I personally (and most of the people here) would have preferred that the old order be overthrown and the new more quickly constructed. Today's children, perhaps, will live another, better life. No chance of that for me and those older than me.

And yet, I am finding reassurance. Fortunately, I'm not fifty and have not lived out my best years in that crushing bad faith and cynicism in which my parents, for example, were forced to live. They, and many others, survived, although many were broken, not having endured morally. Worst of all is to be seventy years old. Imagine: to have lived a lifetime under the Soviet regime and, in old age, to feel that all been wasted, all a mistake, a blind alley.

There's another possible model of the near future: an aggravated economic crisis, general strikes, the shutting down of the large factories and the transportation system, and then the final attempt at bringing order with a "firm hand" and preserving the "great state." Perhaps even a dictatorship of the right, for a brief time, after which everything will collapse, utterly. Personally, I believe more in the slow model. We'll see.

It's not easy to be living now, during the disintegration of this wretched but still powerful old order. I would really like to convince you of this. Perhaps because I know your optimism, or maybe because subconsciously I want some normal human sympathy.

March 28

As you see, Bohdan, this epilogue isn't coming out all in one piece.

Today, all of Kiev once again has its heart in its mouth, following the goings-on in Moscow. Two days ago, Gorbachev forbade all demonstrations and rallies in the streets for two weeks. The problem is that "Democratic Russia" had planned an enormous rally, timed to coincide with the opening of the extraordinary congress of people's deputies of the RSFSR. And the Center, panicking and in hysterics, decided to ban it. Formally, the ban was a response to an appeal to President Gorbachev from a couple of dozen Russian deputies to protect them from an assault by the crowd which was gathering on Red Square at the time of the session. There were also rumors that the Russian communists, in a parallel move, were going to demand Yeltsin's resignation. Today Moscow is crammed with soldiers and military hardware, the Kremlin is under siege, the deputies have gone to their meeting through a cordon of militia and riot police. Manège Square, where all the rallies are held, has been blocked off; the atmosphere is explosive and fraught with danger. The war between Russia and the Union, a battle of the titans, has reached its apogee.

Kiev is holding its collective breath: all who can do so are phoning Moscow with one question: "Well, how are things up there?" During the day, we learned that Gorbachev has promised to withdraw the army and police tomorrow. In the meantime, the congress quit, refusing to work under siege. And, in the evening, a rally was held within a circle of soldiers.

It's been impossible to buy bread in Kiev for two days now. The neighborhood bread stores have simply shut up shop, and at those which have stayed open enormous queues have formed all day long. I've seen something like this only in the movies; now for the first time I see the real thing. A striking picture. Surly people. Yesterday metal workers struck in support of the miners' demands. The miners have decided to fight to the end, and the aggressive stance of the central government toward the strikers is only embittering people. Today it appears that the first, slow model of our future isn't going to work. Some leaders of the Russian democratic movement are predicting complete economic collapse within five months.

April 2

A dramatic confrontation in Moscow was somehow averted. The March 28 rally took place—more than 700,000 people showed up. During these last few days, everyone who retains even a modicum of interest in politics has been watching the battles at the Russian congress—the dramatic struggle of Yeltsin and his team against the Union.

Against this background, Kiev's parliamentary life seems almost calm.

The communists have quieted down since the referendum, and the democrats are going into battle not quite so inflamed. Only in Lviv have the democrats enthusiastically celebrated the anniversary of their coming to power. It was a year ago in March that the first parliamentary elections in the history of Ukraine were held. I was in Edmonton then, and you and I, unbelievably excited, telephoned Kiev to find out who had won and who lost.

The new state prices, fixed by the Center (this is what our pseudo-market à la Gorbachev looks like) and in effect as of today, are so outrageously steep that they defile all the stale promises for some kind of happiness and well-being in one's future life. In the end, no one believes any more in that happiness and well-being. Not the intellectuals, not I or my colleagues: it's a blow above all to our hopes of travel in the

West. A ticket to North America now costs more than 6,000 rubles. So, you're free to leave the country, but just try to get out with such ticket prices and the total shortage of tickets, even at today's prices. Even at the new prices, people are lining up; but they're gloomier now, as the newspapers are more sarcastic. And everyone, as always, as every day in the last while, is thinking about the future. What's going to happen tomorrow?

Maybe no one knows the answer to this question, neither the coal miners with their desperate political demand for the resignation of the President, nor the partocrats with their stubborn wish to defend our famished "socialist choice," nor the quixotic oppositionists, nor the closeted intellectuals. Nor do I know what's going to happen to us all tomorrow and to this state (there is no prospect for a state under the rubric of "USSR"), but I am sure it will be something different than what we had yesterday. Where there is movement of some sort, there is some kind of hope.

All the best.

Notes

1. Taras Shevchenko (1814-61). Born a serf, he became Ukraine's greatest poet and national hero. Persecuted by the tsarist regime for his political, social and national views, he personified Ukraine's struggle for freedom.

2. Borys Oliinyk, 59, poet, long-time head of the Ukrainian Writers' Union party organization who published vicious attacks on Rukh and its leaders, Dmytro Pavlychko in particular. Elected to the USSR Congress of People's Deputies in 1989 from the quota of 100 seats allocated to the Communist party, he became deputy chairman of the Council of Nationalities and a firm supporter of Gorbachev's policies. After the failed putsch of August 1991 and the proclamation of Ukraine's independence, he disappeared from the political scene.

3. Dmytro Pavlychko, 61, poet, member of the Rukh leadership and first head the Ukrainian Language Society. He was elected to the USSR Congress of People's Deputies in 1989 and in 1990 to Ukraine's parliament. As chairman of the Ukrainian parliament's Standing Commission on Foreign Relations and member of its Presidium, he plays a key role in formulating Ukraine's foreign policy.

4. Ivan Dziuba, 61, literary critic. He was imprisoned during the 1960s for his work *Internationalism or Russification?* (London, 1968). One of Ukraine's best known intellectuals, in 1990 he was elected the first president of the Republican Association of Ukrainian Studies.

5. The term *samizdat* (*samvydav* in Ukrainian) means self-publishing and refers to the unofficial reproduction and circulation of uncensored written materials. Until 1988, these materials were in typescript form, since individuals and groups were denied access to printing facilities. Thereafter some independent

organizations started publishing bulletins, newspapers and magazines which were called "unofficial publications." After changes in press regulations and the banning of the Communist party in August 1991, the distinction between "official" and "unofficial" publications lost relevance.

6. The blue-and-yellow flag was banned in Soviet Ukraine, since it was the identified with the national movement that fought for Ukraine's independence during the 1917 revolution. The official flag of the republic was red, with a blue stripe. The democratic movement in Ukraine adopted the blue-and-yellow flag, and this banner was declared the national flag on August 24, 1991 in connection with Ukraine's Proclamation of Independence. On January 28, 1992, it became the official state flag.

7. Rukh (the word means "movement") is Ukraine's people's front and the main democratic opposition force. In November 1988 the Kiev branch of the Writers' Union of Ukraine and the Institute of Literature joined forces to form an initiative committee to launch a people's front. The September 1989 Rukh constituent congress was attended by 1,109 delegates representing 280,000 members. Originally called the "People's Movement in Support of Restructuring in Ukraine," in 1991 the name was changed to "People's Movement of Ukraine" (*Narodnyi rukh Ukrainy*).

8. Viacheslav Briukhovetsky, 44, literary scholar and one of the founders of Rukh, was appointed Rector of the Kievan-Mohyla Academy in 1991. A leading center of scholarship in the Slavic world, the Academy was closed almost two centuries ago by the tsarist regime and will re-open its doors in September 1992.

9. The Ukrainian Supreme Rada (Soviet) is Ukraine's parliament. It is unicameral and has 450 deputies. Until the March 1990 elections, it played no substantial role in Ukrainian politics. Parliament is presided over by the "head" (*holova*) or chairman, who is assisted by two deputy heads. Together with the chairmen of the 24 standing commissions of parliament, these officials form the Presidium, which can issue decrees between sessions of Parliament. Members of the Council of Ministers (renamed the Cabinet of Ministers in 1990) are ratified by parliament and do not have to be deputies. Following the 1990

elections, the opposition held one-third of the seats in parliament, while the communists controlled 239 votes. The disintegration of the communist bloc in parliament began in the spring of 1991, when on many occasions some 100 communists would vote with the opposition. In today's Supreme Rada, the lines of division between factions are not clear, since in addition to various political groupings (with overlapping membership) there exist blocs representing various group interests (for example, agriculturalists and factory directors).

10. The Taras Shevchenko Ukrainian Language Society inaugural congress took place in February 1989. Since it was dedicated to reviving the Ukrainian language and culture, communist officials hoped to steer the society clear of politics. However, the society supported Rukh and became a collective member of it. With 70,000 members by mid-1989, it was the second largest non-official organization in Ukraine. In November 1991, after Ukraine's declaration of independence and the adoption of Ukrainian as the state language, the organization changed its name to the Prosvita (Enlightenment) society, reflecting the new focus on popular education.

11. Symon Petliura (1879-1926), social democrat who was a major figure in Ukraine's independence movement during the years 1917-21. A member of the Central Rada, Ukraine's first independent government, he was commander-in-chief of the Ukrainian National Republic's armed forces during the chaos and anarchy that engulfed Ukraine in 1919-20, one of the worst aspects of which was widespread pogroms. He was assassinated in exile in Paris by Shalom Schwarzbard, allegedly in retaliation for the massacre of Jews perpetrated by UNR forces. Petliura was favorably disposed towards Jews and Jewish-Ukrainian cooperation. The historical debate centers on whether he was active enough in preventing pogroms by groups that avowed loyalty to the UNR. In general the UNR government did not exert effective control over such groups. Considerable controversy surrounds the relative role of Whites, Reds and Ukrainian groups in perpetrating pogroms. The Soviet authorities conducted an active campaign to attribute all pogroms to the pro-UNR forces.

12. Levko Lukianenko, 65, lawyer and former political prisoner who spent more than 26 years in the gulag. Elected to parliament in 1990, he heads the Ukrainian Republican Party and was its candidate in the 1991 presidential elections. (He obtained 1.4 million votes, or 4.9 per cent of the total.) In 1961 he was arrested for organizing the Ukrainian Workers' and Peasants' Union, a small group committed to democracy and independence. Although he was condemned to death, his sentence was commuted to 15 years' imprisonment. Released in 1975, he was rearrested in 1977 for his membership in the Ukrainian Helsinki Group and returned to Ukraine in 1989.

13. The Ukrainian Republican Party was founded in April 1990 on the basis of the Ukrainian Helsinki Union. In 1991 it had some 5,000 members.

14. Volodymyr Ivashko, 60. Appointed first secretary of the Communist Party of Ukraine in September 1989, he was elected head of the Supreme Rada in May 1990. On July 11, 1990, in the midst of the intense political debate over Ukraine's Declaration of Sovereignty, Ivashko resigned his Ukrainian posts and moved to Moscow to become deputy general secretary of the Communist Party of the Soviet Union, a post he held until the collapse of the party in August 1992.

15. Yurii Badzio, 55, literary critic and former dissident. Arrested in 1979, he returned to Ukraine from the gulag in 1988. In December 1990 he was elected head of the Democratic party of Ukraine.

16. Ukrainian Helsinki Union, launched officially in March 1988 as a continuation of the Ukrainian Public Group to Promote the Implementation of the Helsinki Accords, which had been established in November 1976 with some 40 members. By 1980 three-fourths of the members of the Ukrainian Public Group were imprisoned, with sentences ranging from ten to fifteen years. The remainder were exiled from Ukraine or, to appease foreign opinion, allowed to emigrate. Levko Lukianenko was elected the first head of the Ukrainian Helsinki Union and, in April 1990, the union voted to transform itself into the Ukrainian Republican party.

17. Viacheslav Chornovil, 54, journalist and one of Ukraine's best-known dissidents, author of *The Chornovil Papers* (London, 1968). First arrested in 1967, he was rearrested twice and spent more than ten years in labor camps and exile. A member of the Ukrainian Public Group to Promote the Implementation of the Helsinki Accords, he returned to Lviv in 1985. In March 1990, he was elected deputy to Ukraine's parliament and the following month chairman of the Lviv Oblast Council. He was Rukh's candidate in the December 1991 presidential elections and received 7.4 million votes (or 23.2 per cent of the total).

18. The Democratic Bloc was formed in November 1989 under Rukh's auspices to contest the March 1990 elections. It regrouped some 43 different organizations. Rukh could not participate in the elections directly, because authorities procrastinated with registration procedures until the deadline for the nomination of candidates had passed. In the March 1990 elections the Democratic Bloc candidates won 117 seats in the Supreme Rada, as did 71 candidates supported by the Bloc. The Bloc won majorities in the Galician oblasts and many key cities, among them Kiev. In June 1990, the Democratic Bloc deputies in parliament constituted themselves as an opposition caucus called Narodna Rada or People's Council.

19. Leonid Kravchuk was elected President of Ukraine in December 1991 with a 61.6 per cent majority. In July 1990 he was elected head of Ukraine's Parliament. A lecturer in political economy, from 1960 he worked in various posts within the Communist Party of Ukraine apparatus, rising to the rank of second secretary for ideology, in which capacity he was the party's chief public opponent of Rukh. In 1990, he was briefly second secretary of the party's Central Committee.

20. Ivan Pliushch, 50, was elected head of Ukraine's parliament in December 1991. As the first deputy head of parliament when the body was chaired by Leonid Kravchuk, he became a favorite of the democratic opposition because of his advocacy of Ukraine's independence and of democratic and economic reform.

21. Genrikh Altunian, 59, a military engineer who was arrested in 1969 and sentenced to three years in labor camps for member-

ship in the Initiative Group for the Defense of Human Rights in the USSR.

22. Pavlo Movchan, 53, poet, and one of Rukh's founders, was elected head of the Ukrainian Language Society (Prosvita) in November 1991.

23. Ivan Drach, 56, poet, head of the Board of the Kiev Writers' Union and head of Rukh. A collection of his early poetry (*Orchard Lamps*, New York, 1978) was edited and introduced by Stanley Kunitz.

24. Mykhailo Horyn, 61, an educator and psychologist, was first arrested in 1966 and sentenced to six years in a labor camp. In 1981 he was sentenced to ten years in the gulag and five years of internal exile. Released in 1985, he became a leading figure in Rukh and heads its political council. He is chairman of Parliament's Sub-Commission for Relations with Ukrainians outside the Boundaries of Ukraine.

25. Ihor Yukhnovsky, 67, physicist, head of the parliamentary standing Commission on Science and Education and member of the Presidium, led the opposition, the *Narodna Rada*, until January 1992. He was a candidate of the Party of Democratic Renaissance in the December 1991 presidential elections and obtained 555,000 votes (or 1.7 per cent of the total).

26. Banderism, an integral-nationalist ideology associated with Stepan Bandera, who led the Organization of Ukrainian Nationalists (OUN). The OUN emerged in the 1930s in Polish-held Galicia and during the Second World War led the Ukrainian Insurgent Army (UPA), a partisan formation that fought both Nazi and Soviet occupation troops. Stepan Bandera was assassinated in Munich in 1959 by a KGB agent. The tendency of Soviet authorities to label all those upholding Ukraine's national rights "Banderites" only enhanced the popularity of this term. However, indicative of the real strength of the integral-nationalist current in Ukraine (called the Inter-Party Assembly) is the fact that it failed to gather the 100,000 signatures needed to register a candidate in the 1991 presidential elections.

27. The Ukrainian Autocephalous (Self-governed) Orthodox church was established in 1921, thus reviving the independence of the church that was lost in 1686, when tsarist authorities subordinated the Ukrainian Orthodox church to the Moscow Patriarch. The Autocephalous church was suppressed by the Soviet regime in 1930. Most of its bishops and priests were either executed or sent to labor camps, and its parishes were given to the Russian Orthodox church, which was the only Orthodox church permitted. In February 1989 the Autocephalous church was launched in Kiev with the support of Rukh and other democratic forces. By February 1990 it had seven bishops and more than 200 priests and in June elevated Mstyslav, Metropolitan of the American Ukrainian Orthodox church, to the office of autocephalous Patriarch of Kiev.

28. The Russian Orthodox church in Ukraine was the pro-regime church. In 1990 it renamed itself the Ukrainian Orthodox church, and in December 1991, following the declaration of independence, took steps to establish its autocephaly from Moscow.

29. Leopold Taburiansky, 52, deputy in Ukraine's parliament and head of the Olymp cooperative, ran for president in the December 1991 elections and obtained 183,000 votes (0.6 per cent of the total).

30. The Central Rada was the revolutionary parliament formed in March 1917 that directed the Ukrainian national movement and with its four universals (government manifestos) led Ukraine from autonomy to independence in January 1918.

31. Oleksandr Savchenko, 34, was appointed deputy governor of Ukraine's central bank in 1991.

32. A Union of Democratic City and Oblast Councils (Radas) was established and elected Serhii Konev as its chairman. The union is one of Ukraine's most important democratic organizations.

33. Colonel Vilen Martyrosian, 52, an Armenian deputy in the USSR Congress of Deputies from Rivne, may be considered one of the founding fathers of Ukraine's independent armed forces. In spring 1991, the first congress of the Ukrainian Officers' Union,

a grass-roots movement organized by Rukh, elected him head of the union. In January 1992 he was appointed chairman of the Cabinet of Ministers' Committee on the Social Welfare of the Armed Forces of Ukraine.

34. Bohdan Horyn, 56, brother of Mykhailo Horyn, a scholar working in art and literature, was sentenced in 1966 to four years in labor camp. As deputy chairman of parliament's Commission on Foreign Relations, he plays an important role in the formulation of Ukraine's foreign policy.

35. October Revolution Square was renamed Independence Square in September 1990.

36. A *kobzar* was a wandering folk bard who performed a large repertoire of historical epic songs, accompanying himself on a kobza or bandura.

37. Volodymyr Vynnychenko (1880-1951), writer and social democratic political leader who in 1917 headed the Secretariat of the Central Rada, Ukraine's first independent government.

38. Ivan Mazepa (1639-1709), hetman of Ukraine, whose attempt to throw off Russian domination ended in defeat by the forces of tsar Peter I in the Battle of Poltava (1709).

39. The Ministry of Defense was established in 1991 and is headed by Colonel-General Konstantin Morozov.

40. The Ukrainian Catholic church, also known as the Uniate church, follows the Byzantine rite and was the dominant faith in Western Ukraine until the Soviet occupation of this region. In 1946 the Uniate church was banned and its clergy forced either to enter the Russian Orthodox church or face imprisonment. The Ukrainian Catholics survived as a church of the catacombs with a clandestine hierarchy. In 1989, 600 Ukrainian Catholic parishes applied for registration, with more than 200 priests of the Russian Orthodox church defecting to the Catholics. In 1991 Cardinal Liubachivsky arrived from Rome to head the church. Throughout 1990 there was tension in Western Ukraine, fueled by the communist apparatus, as some former priests of the

Russian Orthodox church joined the Ukrainian Autocephalous Orthodox church, while others joined the Ukrainian Catholic church. By the end of 1991 tension subsided as democratic mechanisms were put in place to resolve parish disputes.

41. Solomea Pavlychko's prediction was off by two months. The demolition of the grotesque Lenin monument on Independence Square (formerly October Revolution Square) began in September 1991.

42. Yurii Shcherbak, 58, deputy of the USSR Congress of People's Deputies, medical doctor and writer, author of *Chernobyl: A Documentary Story* (London, 1989), became State Minister of the Environment in 1991.

43. Zviad Gamsakhurdia won the 1991 presidential elections in Georgia by a landslide. He proved to be an authoritarian figure and in 1992 was deposed in bloody civil strife.

44. The saga of Stepan Khmara continued throughout most of 1991. In July 1991 he was rearrested in his hotel for refusing to recognize the legality of the court trying his case. The matter was resolved in August, when charges against him were dropped and Procurator-General Potebenko, who initiated the case, was replaced by the democrat Shyshkin. In independent Ukraine, Khmara has emerged as an active member of the Standing Committee on Defense and Security.

45. In Russian-ruled Ukraine, the 1917 revolution culminated with the proclamation of a Ukrainian National Republic on January 22, 1918. In the territories formerly under Austrian rule, the Western Ukrainian National Republic was proclaimed on November 14, 1918. On January 22, 1919, the unification of both republics was declared in Kiev. Both the act of independence and act of unification were pronounced in St. Sophia's Cathedral Square. On January 22, 1990, Rukh organized its largest mass action: a human chain extending from St. Sophia's Square in Kiev to Lviv. The January 22 anniversary was officially celebrated for the first time in 1992, with President Kravchuk attending a rally in St. Sophia's Square.